Approaches
for GCSE English

Peter Thomas

Shakespeare
Page and Stage

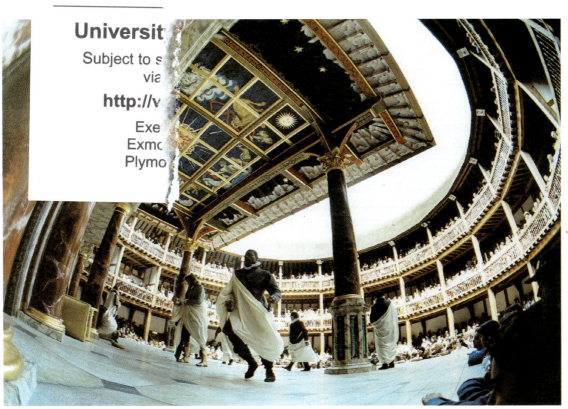

'Julius Caesar' at the Globe Theatre, 1999.

Acknowledgements

The Publisher would like to acknowledge and thank the following
sources for illustrations listed below.

Dominic Photography: © Catherine Ashmore: 23, 36, 129, 141;
© Zoe Dominic: 14, 17, 116; © Richard H. Smith: 38, 55, 83;
e. t. archive: 4, 6, 12, 24, 39, 49, 61, 66, 91, 98, 121; © News Groups
Newspapers/Richard Pohle: title page; Performing Arts Library:
© Clive Barda: 99, 103; © Henrietta Butler: 73, 130, 144.

Pearson Education Limited
Edinburgh Gate
Harlow
Essex
CM20 2JE

England and Associated Companies throughout the World

© Pearson Education Limited 1999

ISBN 0-582-41990-5

First published 1999

Printed in Italy by G. Canale & C. S.p.A.

The Publisher's policy is to use paper manufactured from
sustainable forests.

Contents

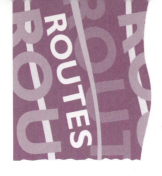

Introduction

Shakespeare, page and stage

Shakespeare has been studied in school for years, but it's only recently that all school students have had to study Shakespeare as part of their English course. The National Curriculum requires all students to study some Shakespeare at Key Stage 3 and for GCSE. How much you study, and which play you study, depends on your teacher, who will decide what suits your class best.

For a long time, studying Shakespeare meant reading the whole play aloud in class. This was fine if everyone understood what they were reading, and read it fluently with interesting expression. It was not so good if readers mumbled or kept stopping at difficult words or the teacher kept interrupting to explain. Reading plays aloud is better than reading them silently, but plays need to be seen as well as heard. Dialogue needs to be linked with action, so that we can watch the situation created by speech between people. The best way to get to grips with a play is to watch a performance of it on the stage. If you don't get a chance to see Shakespeare performed on stage, make sure you see your GCSE Shakespeare text performed on video, especially if you can find two different versions to compare.

This student guide will help you to enjoy a play as a performance script, rather than as a reading book. The activities based on the scripts will help you to think about how Shakespeare's lines should sound, and how actors should perform them on stage. That does not mean it is a book about acting. It's not a Drama book but a book that helps you to make your Shakespeare work different from your work on poetry or prose.

Shakespeare never thought of himself as a writer to be studied for exams. He was an entertainer, someone who wrote to pull in a paying audience, many of whom could not read and write. In his day he was as popular as any TV series is today. Some of the stories in his plays he made up himself, but mostly he adapted popular stories or events that people would have heard of. He spent his whole working life in London, writing for his living, and he was so successful that he was able to retire to a large house in Stratford-upon-Avon where he had grown up.

As a writer of popular performance scripts, Shakespeare knew what appealed to people in the theatre. They liked jokes about sex, and about relations between men and women; jokes about foreigners and their habits; jokes about people in particular jobs, such as pub landlords, farmers or sailors. His plays are full of people, habits and customs which an audience could recognise and laugh at. Although some things have changed since Shakespeare's day – population, electricity, air transport, words, for example – other things are exactly as they were when he was alive. You (or someone you know) will sometimes get jealous, fall in love, dream of being powerful, misunderstand a situation or face up to some test of your morals or principles. These are the things that Shakespeare writes about.

Human behaviour hasn't changed much since Shakespeare's time, even if clothes have changed. We don't wear doublet and hose today, but we can still makes jokes about people who wear anoraks or Armani. We may not make jokes about ostlers and franklins, but we laugh at comedians' jokes about shop assistants or taxi drivers. There are people like Falstaff alive today, gross, idle, lazy drinkers who tell tall stories and try to impress women, especially those who have money. There are circumstances today in which someone may, like Isabella, face a situation where doing something they think is very wrong is the only way to help someone. Relations between men and women will always, perhaps, involve the battles, doubts and differences we see between Beatrice and Benedick and Petruchio and Katharina. And surely, politicians will always be as subtle and devious as Shakespeare shows them in the extracts from *Julius Caesar* and *Coriolanus*.

Shakespeare was an entertainer who used his plays to make people think about moral issues below the surface of daily life. He wasn't a preacher, though. He wanted to make them think and feel, rather than to tell them *how* they should think of feel.

Shakespeare knew that an audience needed variety. Too much seriousness or sadness and gloom would spoil an evening, so he made sure his plays were a mix of moods and plots and characters. There are comic bits in his tragedies and sad bits in his comedies. What made him such a good writer of plays was this blend of ingredients. This is true of his characters too. His heroes and heroines are not clear-cut, successful, decent people. All of them have something wrong with them, particularly the men. And his villains are not simply evil and wicked and hateful. All of them have something endearing or interesting about them. It's as if he thought that in real life nobody is all perfect and nobody is all bad, so he tried to show human beings on the stage who were as mixed in their qualities as people are in real life. Earlier dramatists had kept to the idea that plays should show heroic heroes and villainous villains, with Good coming out the winner. Shakespeare didn't think that was what happened in real life, so he tried to be more realistic in his scripts.

This book concentrates on extracts from a number of plays which show Shakespeare's qualities as a play-writer. All of them can be discussed in class – and some of them are very suitable for performing in class. Some scenes can be played for laughs; others can be played to make us wonder about ourselves and the people around us. The extracts show Shakespeare's insight into comic character and situation, relationships between men and women, difficult judgements and the workings of politics.

When you read the scripts and begin to think of them on stage, it may help to remember some important facts about the stage and the theatre in Shakespeare's day.

Performance in Shakespeare's day

Shakespeare didn't write stage directions in his scripts. The scripts that have come down to us are nearly all copies of the actors' scripts rather than his own director's script. These often contained only the specific actor's lines and cues, in case they fell into the wrong hands and a rival company put the play together and stole the audience. So you won't find many directions in the margin of his scripts, other than "*enter with a flourish*". He inserted subtle directions in a character's speech such as "what bloody man is that" where a more modern writer may write as a stage direction "*Enter a man covered in blood as from a battle*".

The original Globe Theatre painted by J. C. Visscher.

Shakespeare's theatre

Most of the London theatres were on the south bank of the River Thames, outside the rules of the city of London. This was because theatres had gained a bad reputation – they encouraged people to take time off work, and they brought together crowds of people from different places, which meant that germs and disease could spread quickly.

For most of Shakespeare's life, he wrote for an open-air theatre where the wealthiest people could pay for a seat, but others could choose to pay less and stand up. If you can, visit the replica of the Globe or look at some pictures of it to see how these conditions may have affected performance.

Shakespeare didn't have modern aids such as microphones, lighting, moveable sets, mechanically operated curtains or any other devices to show a different setting. Actors needed big voices to ensure that they were heard, and audiences had to accept that the scene had changed when an actor said "This castle hath a pleasant seat" or "So here is the forest at last". Usually the end of a scene was indicated by a pair of rhyming lines, rather than by a curtain closing or lights going down.

Women's parts were acted by boy actors. This could make love scenes difficult, but most of Shakespeare's love scenes involve talk rather than action, which must have been a relief to the actors!

Shakespeare and other actors shared in the profits of their acting company, so it was important to keep coming up with plays that brought in paying audiences. Shakespeare wrote plays to suit audiences who liked romances, historical events, weepy stories and plays full of comic characters and comic scenes. In other words, he made it his business to appeal to every kind of theatregoer so that they would pay to see his plays rather than the plays at the theatre down the road.

Shakespeare's audience

Sometimes Shakespeare wrote plays to be performed indoors at the royal court or a private house, where he could expect his audience to be educated and interested in philosophical ideas. The majority of his plays, though, were written for the public theatre, which was the equivalent of a cinema today. Most of the people who watched his plays were uneducated. They wanted to laugh, to be surprised, to see some action, some passion and some violence. They wanted to be entertained. Shakespeare gave them all this. And he made them think, too, about war and politics, about moral issues and religion, and about poverty, old age, jealousy and ambition.

Using this book for your GCSE

Your work in GCSE will be assessed for a number of things:

1 Knowledge of what happens and familiarity with details.

2 Understanding of:
   - characters' ideas, feelings and attitudes
   - Shakespeare's ideas, feelings and attitudes
   - language and meaning
   - social, cultural and historical aspects
   - Shakespeare's stagecraft (his skill in writing for performance in the theatre).

3 Response to characters, relationships, situations, ideas, feelings and attitudes.

The sections that accompany the Shakespeare scripts are designed to make you familiar with the text and with the skills and knowledge needed for your GCSE. Every script in this book has the same pattern of guidance and support material.
It's worth getting familiar with this pattern.

Introduction

This tells you something about the script and the play from which it has been taken. The scripts are chosen as good examples of Shakespeare's dramatic skill and range of ideas. You may want to follow up the information in the introductions and read more of the play.

Script

The scripts have been slightly edited but these are not simplified versions of the text. Some lines by characters who are not essential to the scene have been removed, and some lines which are obscure and need too much explanation have been cut. The cuts are similar to those that a director might make to give an audience the best version for clear understanding and enjoyment.

Postscript

This is a brief reminder of the three essential elements: what Shakespeare wanted to do, how he did it and the impact on an audience. Usually, his purpose is to entertain but sometimes it is to explore an idea or a moral problem – such as a choice of doing something bad for a result that is good. Effects are reactions by a live audience to what it sees. Devices are the methods used to produce effects, such as asides, soliloquies, disguises and concealments behind the arras (a hanging wall-covering) or a convenient bush.

Shakespeare used a number of theatrical devices, most of which are still used by writers of plays and sitcoms today. Here is a list of some common devices that you can look for when you are thinking about Shakespeare's stagecraft.

Visual devices
- unknown identity
- mistaken identity
- gender swap
- twins
- disguise
- mistaken situation
- dramatic irony (when the audience sees more than the character on stage)
- props and costumes

Aural devices
- overhearing
- mishearing
- aside
- soliloquy (character speaks out loud alone on stage)
- dramatic irony
- malapropism (getting words wrong)
- national stereotype and accent
- parody (mocking imitation)
- puns

Narrative devices

- Chorus to explain and link
- dialogue used to describe non-staged events
- dialogue used to introduce an unseen character
- letters and reports

Directorial devices

- sound cues to an actor to help expression (sibilants – "S" sounds; plosives – "P" or "B" sounds; fricatives "K" or "G" sounds; vowels); Short vowels show urgency. Long vowels show lament.
- action cues to other actors ("Do not wave your hat so")
- cues to audience ("I'll hide behind this bush and listen")

Structural devices

- act structure – e.g. setting; arrivals; dilemma; effects; resolution
- scene structure – varying mood, plot, setting, character
- scene parallel
- scene contrast
- plots and sub-plots

Stylistic devices

- characterisation in speech (idiom – accent – repeated phrases – errors)
- verse/prose (status – important people/speeches in verse, common people/ordinary dialogue in prose)
- imagery (cue audience by using simile and metaphor)
- rhetorical questions – parody – alliteration patterns

Audience-appeal devices

- pleasing the "groundlings" (verbal abuse, drunkenness)
- pleasing the educated (puns, parodies, conceits)
- dance (interlude, variety, spectacle)
- song (interlude, variety)
- contemporary references
- slapstick/farce
- dramatic irony

Glossary

This is to explain words which are unfamiliar or have changed their meaning. Also, using the glossary is a very good way to see how language and life have changed since Shakespeare's time. It helps you to find material for comments on social, cultural and historical aspects of your work.

Close-up on language

This is not a long or detailed section, but a quick reference to one or two features of language that can be seen in the script.

Understanding character

This section gets you to empathise with the characters, whether you like them or not. The point of looking at moments in the text when a character is thinking something or feeling something is to help you to read for implied meaning as well as explicit meaning. Sometimes, what the character is thinking and feeling is clear from what the character *says*, but sometimes the character's real thoughts and feelings may be different from what they say. This may be because the character is hiding a thought or a feeling. It may also be because they don't know something that the audience knows, and say something that has more meaning than they realise, or has a very different meaning from the one they think it has.

Personal response

You will have your own reactions to characters, to ideas, to attitudes or to situations and relationships. You should be able to say what you think and feel, and why you think and feel the way you do.

Understanding performance

Some of the scripts are very easily performed in the classroom – the Falstaff scripts and the *Much Ado About Nothing* scripts for example. Others, such as *The Merchant of Venice*, are less easy to perform in the classroom, but pose dilemmas for a director. This section asks you to think about the actor playing the character and about how to direct tone, pause, gesture and movement around the stage.

Tone

- angry
- arrogant
- accusing
- begging
- challenging
- commanding
- confident
- denying
- disbelieving
- excusing
- frightened
- nervous
- passionate
- shocked
- pleading
- questioning
- tender
- uncertain
- weary…

Think how a simple line may be made different by using a different tone:

"I think you should go." (Try commanding, then tender.)

"You and I must sort this out." (Try angry, then weary.)

Pause

Sometimes a vast difference can be made by pausing after or before a word, or even before starting to say something in answer to a question.

Try this: "I think your new top is very nice." Compare this: "I think your new top is (pause) very nice." What is the difference?

Try "What on earth is that thing?" compared with "What on earth is that (pause) thing?"

Gesture

Here are twenty gestures that can be used by characters in scripts in this book: you could practise each of these and check with a partner what each gesture suggests about the speaker or the listener:

- adjusting clothing (straightening tie/smoothing skirt/brushing sleeve)
- avoiding direct eye contact
- looking around to see if anyone is listening
- pointing to an object or person
- putting a hand on one's heart
- putting an arm around the shoulder
- putting a hand over one's mouth
- rubbing hands together
- showing someone the door
- showing two open hands
- shrugging shoulders
- tapping fingers
- thumping a desk
- touching hands
- turning one's back to someone
- twiddling thumbs
- waving someone to a seat
- whispering into someone's ear
- winking
- wiping a tear from one's eye.

Movement

Remember to use the whole stage, rather than standing still to deliver your lines. Think about when you might move:

- to the front of the stage near the audience
- to the back of the stage
- to the side of the stage
- towards a speaker or listener
- away from a speaker or listener
- in a brisk, hurried way
- slowly and uncertainly.

Practical work

The most important thing you can do with Shakespeare's scripts is to try them out. Some of the scripts are very easy to perform and to improvise. You will understand Shakespeare best when you treat him as a writer for performance, and this doesn't need brilliant acting ability or fancy theatre kit. Your classroom can suddenly become like an Elizabethan theatre if you play the scene with a huge Falstaff squeezing into a laundry basket to hide from an angry husband, and two revengeful women taking the opportunity to pile dirty washing on top of him. Get together, ease up and have some fun. Shakespeare would prefer you to laugh and think rather than treat him as a part of an examination duty.

Social, cultural and historical aspects

There are two ways of looking at this. The simplest is to find examples in the scripts of attitudes and behaviour that tell us how people lived in Shakespeare's day. For example, the beginning of 'Falstaff the great fighter' in Chapter 2 has a scene where merchants and farmers are getting up early in the morning to travel to London. We learn about the sort of goods they took to market, how they carried them, what it was like to stay in a hostelry and what sort of dangers there were on the road. (You will certainly need to use the glossary for this, as words such as "bots" and "long-staff sixpenny striker" have disappeared from the language.)

Another – and sometimes more interesting – approach to this section is to ask what the scripts tell us about our culture and society today. If, for example, we disapprove of the way Petruchio treats Katharina in *The Taming of the Shrew*, is this because our attitude to sexism today is different from Shakespeare's? If we feel uneasy about the behaviour of the Christians in *The Merchant of Venice*, is this because we have different attitudes to racism because we know how it resulted in the horrors of the Holocaust?

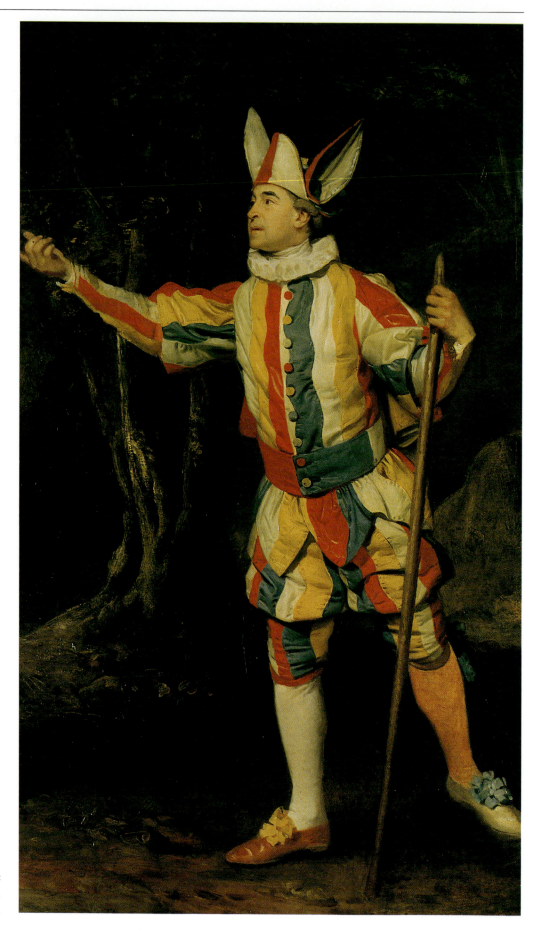

*Thomas King as Touchstone in
'As You Like It' in 1767.
Painted by Zoffany.*

If you are looking in the texts for clues to the social, cultural and historical features of Shakespeare's time, you can check out any of these:

Attitudes
- to God
- to war
- to duty
- to witchcraft
- to monarchy
- to women
- to foreigners

Ideas
- about science
- about reason
- about justice
- about government
- about human nature

Language
- words that are unfamiliar or have changed their meaning
- oaths and words used to insult and abuse
- expressions derived from jobs and experiences that don't exist any more
- differences in word order

Conditions
- plague
- foreign discoveries
- entertainment
- farming
- seafaring

Events
- Spanish wars
- treason
- battles
- civil wars
- royal occasion

Stage conditions
- open
- no curtains
- no copyright
- no sound amplification
- no set changes
- rival companies
- no lighting
- no extras

Finally, this book is designed to bring together the three parts of the GCSE triangle: Shakespeare, you and your English work. The first two are the important ones. If you and Shakespeare get together closely enough, you'll be a powerful partnership. Get that right and you will be well prepared for the GCSE part of the triangle.

The rustics get ready – from *A Midsummer Night's Dream*

Introduction

The people of Athens have heard that the Duke is to put on a great celebration for his daughter's wedding. Some of them decide to perform a play as part of the big event. The tradesmen who plan this amateur dramatic show are not educated and they are not experienced actors. However, Peter Quince thinks he knows a thing or two, and Bottom the weaver thinks he knows even more.

In these scenes where the amateurs rehearse their play, Shakespeare writes from personal experience about bad acting: these amateurs misread their lines, miss their cues and misunderstand the words of their script. Bottom is so convinced that he is God's gift to acting that he wants to play several parts, and wants to show off his skills and his props and his costumes. Peter Quince, the organiser or director, has a hard time trying to keep this company in order. He's not helped by the fact that the play he has chosen is not the best-written one in the land.

The rehearsal comes to an end when Puck, a fairy, decides to play a trick on the mortals by putting a donkey's head on Bottom.

Maggie Smith in 'A Midsummer Night's Dream', 1977.

Script

Act I, Scene 2

Quince's house

Enter Quince, Snug, Bottom, Flute, Snout, and Starveling

QUINCE: Is all our company here?

BOTTOM: You were best to call them generally, man by man, according to the scrip.

QUINCE: Here is the scroll of every man's name, which is thought fit, through all Athens, to play in our interlude before the duke and the duchess, on his wedding-day at night.

BOTTOM: First, good Peter Quince, say what the play treats on, then read the names of the actors, and so grow to a point.

QUINCE: Marry, our play is, 'The most lamentable comedy, and most cruel death of Pyramus and Thisby'.

BOTTOM: A very good piece of work, I assure you, and a merry. Now, good Peter Quince, call forth your actors by the scroll. Masters, spread yourselves.

QUINCE: Answer as I call you. Nick Bottom, the weaver.

BOTTOM: Ready. Name what part I am for, and proceed.

QUINCE: You, Nick Bottom, are set down for Pyramus.

BOTTOM: What is Pyramus? a lover, or a tyrant?

QUINCE: A lover, that kills himself most gallant for love.

BOTTOM: That will ask some tears in the true performing of it: if I do it, let the audience look to their eyes; I will move storms, I will condole in some measure. To the rest: yet my chief humour is for a tyrant: I could play Ercles rarely, or a part to tear a cat in, to make all split.
'The raging rocks
And shivering shocks
Shall break the locks
Of prison gates;
And Phibbus' car
Shall shine from far
And make and mar
The foolish Fates.'
This was lofty! Now name the rest of the players. This is Ercles' vein, a tyrant's vein; a lover is more condoling.

QUINCE: Francis Flute, the bellows-mender.

FLUTE: Here, Peter Quince.

QUINCE:	Flute, you must take Thisby on you.
FLUTE:	What is Thisby? a wandering knight?
QUINCE:	It is the lady that Pyramus must love.
FLUTE:	Nay, faith, let me not play a woman; I have a beard coming.
QUINCE:	That's all one: you shall play it in a mask, and you may speak as small as you will.
BOTTOM:	An I may hide my face, let me play Thisby too, I'll speak in a monstrous little voice. 'Thisne, Thisne'; 'Ah, Pyramus, my lover dear! Thy Thisby dear, and lady dear!'
QUINCE:	No, no; you must play Pyramus: and, Flute, you Thisby.
BOTTOM:	Well, proceed.
QUINCE:	Robin Starveling, the tailor.
STARVELING:	Here, Peter Quince.
QUINCE:	Robin Starveling, you must play Thisby's mother. Tom Snout, the tinker.
SNOUT:	Here, Peter Quince.
QUINCE:	You, Pyramus' father: myself, Thisby's father: Snug, the joiner; you, the lion's part: and, I hope, here is a play fitted.
SNUG:	Have you the lion's part written? Pray you, if it be, give it me, for I am slow of study.
QUINCE:	You may do it extempore, for it is nothing but roaring.
BOTTOM:	Let me play the lion too: I will roar, that I will do any man's heart good to hear me; I will roar, that I will make the duke say 'Let him roar again, let him roar again.'
QUINCE:	An you should do it too terribly, you would fright the duchess and the ladies, that they would shriek; and that were enough to hang us all.
ALL:	That would hang us, every mother's son.
BOTTOM:	I grant you, friends, if that you should fright the ladies out of their wits, they would have no more discretion but to hang us: but I will aggravate my voice so that I will roar you as gently as any sucking dove; I will roar you an 'twere any nightingale.
QUINCE:	You can play no part but Pyramus; for Pyramus is a sweet-faced man; a proper man, as one shall see in a summer's day; a most lovely gentleman-like man: therefore you must needs play Pyramus.

The dramatic use of costume and lighting is particularly effective in this performance of 'A Midsummer Night's Dream'.
Maggie Smith is centre stage.

BOTTOM: Well, I will undertake it. What beard were I best to
            play it in?

QUINCE: Why, what you will.

BOTTOM: I will discharge it in either your straw-colour beard, your
            orange-tawny beard, your purple-in-grain beard, or
            your French-crown-colour beard, your perfect yellow.

QUINCE: Some of your French crowns have no hair at all, and then
            you will play bare-faced. But, masters, here are your parts:
            and I am to entreat you, request you and desire you, to
            con them by to-morrow night; and meet me in the palace
            wood, a mile without the town, by moonlight; there will
            we rehearse, for if we meet in the city, we shall be dogged
            with company, and our devices known. In the meantime
            I will draw a bill of properties, such as our play wants.
            I pray you, fail me not.

BOTTOM: We will meet; and there we may rehearse most obscenely
            and courageously. Take pains; be perfect: adieu.

QUINCE: At the duke's oak we meet.

BOTTOM: Enough; hold or cut bow-strings.

Exeunt

Act III, Scene 1

In the forest, at the Duke's oak

Enter Quince, Snug, Bottom, Flute, Snout, and Starveling

BOTTOM: Are we all met?

QUINCE: Pat, pat; and here's a marvellous convenient place for
            our rehearsal. This green plot shall be our stage, this
            hawthorn-brake our tiring-house; and we will do it in
            action as we will do it before the duke.

BOTTOM: Peter Quince,—

QUINCE: What sayest thou, bully Bottom?

BOTTOM: There are things in this comedy of Pyramus and Thisby
            that will never please. First, Pyramus must draw a
            sword to kill himself; which the ladies cannot abide.
            How answer you that?

SNOUT: By'r lakin, a parlous fear.

STARVELING: I believe we must leave the killing out, when all is done.

BOTTOM: Not a whit: I have a device to make all well. Write me a
            prologue; and let the prologue seem to say, we will do
            no harm with our swords, and that Pyramus is not
            killed indeed; and, for the more better assurance, tell

them that I, Pyramus, am not Pyramus, but Bottom
the weaver: this will put them out of fear.

QUINCE: Well, we will have such a prologue; and it shall be
written in eight and six.

BOTTOM: No, make it two more; let it be written in eight and eight.

SNOUT: Will not the ladies be afeard of the lion?

STARVELING: I fear it, I promise you.

BOTTOM: Masters, you ought to consider with yourselves: to bring
in – God shield us! – a lion among ladies, is a most
dreadful thing; for there is not a more fearful wild-fowl
than your lion living; and we ought to look to 't.

SNOUT: Therefore another prologue must tell he is not a lion.

BOTTOM: Nay, you must name his name, and half his face must be
seen through the lion's neck: and he himself must speak
through, saying thus, or to the same defect, – 'Ladies,' –
or 'Fair-ladies – I would wish you,' – or 'I would request
you,' – or 'I would entreat you, – not to fear, not to
tremble. If you think I come hither as a lion, it were pity
of my life: no I am no such thing; I am a man as other
men are'; and there indeed let him name his name, and
tell them plainly he is Snug the joiner.

QUINCE: Well it shall be so. But there is two hard things; that is,
to bring the moonlight into a chamber; for, you know,
Pyramus and Thisby meet by moonlight.

SNOUT: Doth the moon shine that night we play our play?

BOTTOM: A calendar, a calendar! look in the almanac; find out
moonshine, find out moonshine.

QUINCE: Yes, it doth shine that night.

BOTTOM: Why, then may you leave a casement of the great
chamber window, where we play, open, and the moon
may shine in at the casement.

QUINCE: Ay; or else one must come in with a bush of thorns and
a lantern, and say he comes to disfigure, or to present,
the person of Moonshine. Then, there is another thing:
we must have a wall in the great chamber; for Pyramus
and Thisby says the story, did talk through the chink of
a wall.

SNOUT: You can never bring in a wall. What say you, Bottom?

BOTTOM: Some man or other must present wall: and let him
have some plaster, or some loam, or some rough-cast
about him, to signify wall; and let him hold his fingers
thus, and through that cranny shall Pyramus and
Thisby whisper.

QUINCE: If that may be, then all is well. Come, sit down, every mother's son, and rehearse your parts. Pyramus, you begin: when you have spoken your speech, enter into that brake: and so every one according to his cue.

Enter Puck behind

PUCK: What hempen home-spuns have we swaggering here, So near the cradle of the fairy queen? What, a play toward! I'll be an auditor; An actor too, perhaps, if I see cause.

QUINCE: Speak, Pyramus. Thisby, stand forth.

BOTTOM: 'Thisby, the flowers of odious savours sweet,'—

QUINCE: Odious? – odorous!

BOTTOM: '—odours savours sweet: So hath thy breath, my dearest Thisby dear. But hark, a voice! stay thou but here awhile, And by and by I will to thee appear.'

Exit

FLUTE: Must I speak now?

QUINCE: Ay, marry, must you; for you must understand he goes but to see a noise that he heard, and is to come again.

FLUTE: 'Most radiant Pyramus, most lily-white of hue, Of colour like the red rose on triumphant brier, Most brisky juvenal and eke most lovely Jew, As true as truest horse that yet would never tire, I'll meet thee, Pyramus, at Ninny's tomb.'

QUINCE: 'Ninus' tomb,' man: why, you must not speak that yet; that you answer to Pyramus: you speak all your part at once, cues and all. Pyramus enter: your cue is past; it is, 'never tire'.

FLUTE: O, – 'As true as truest horse, that yet would never tire.'

Re-enter Puck, and Bottom with an ass's head

BOTTOM: 'If I were fair, Thisby, I were only thine.'

QUINCE: O monstrous! O strange! we are haunted. Pray, masters! fly, masters! Help!

Exeunt Quince, Snug, Flute, Snout, and Starveling

Postscript

Purpose
- entertainment

Effects
- laughter at Bottom's eagerness and bad acting
- laughter at other bad actors
- laughter at Peter Quince's attempts to keep everything and everyone in order

Devices
- parody
- verbal humour
- comical costume

Glossary

lamentable	regrettable, sad
condole	lament, express grief
Ercles	Hercules
Phibbus' car	the sun
condoling	pathetic
extempore	made up on the spot
crowns	coins (and heads)
entreat	beg
con	study
hawthorn-brake	hawthorn bush
tiring-house	dressing room
by'r lakin	By Our Lady
parlous	perilous
eight and six	numbers of syllables in a ballad
casement	window
loam	rough plaster
hempen home-spuns	common people (like common cloth)
odious	hateful, unpleasant
brier	briar
juvenal	juvenile

Close-up on language

1 Find some examples of humour created by characters who misuse words.

2 Find some examples of exaggerated dramatic expression which Shakespeare may have written to mock bad play-writing.

Understanding character

Try to get inside a character's mind. Look at moments where the character reacts to a situation or to someone else and see what the character may be thinking or feeling at that moment. Sometimes the character's thoughts and feelings will be very clear from

Falstaff the great fighter – from *Henry IV Part I*

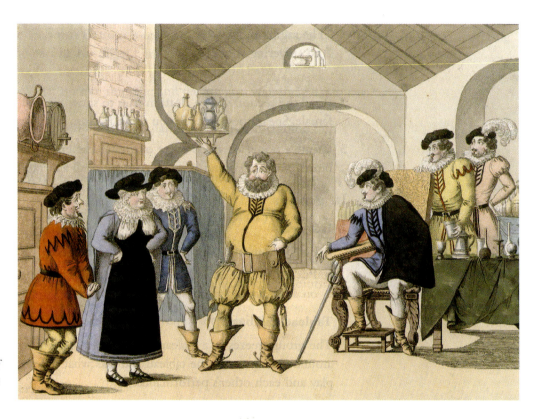

A cartoon of a performance of 'Henry IV' engraved in the 19th century.

Introduction

Prince Henry, known as Hal is the son of King Henry IV. His father expects him to take over the throne and rule as a wise and strong king. For the moment, Hal is displeasing his father by mixing with some low-life characters in East London. These drunkards and thieves are glad to call Hal their friend. The main low-life character, Jack Falstaff, an elderly knight who has spent his life avoiding work and seeking pleasure, thinks all his problems will be solved when Prince Hal becomes king.

In this episode a robbery is planned. The Falstaff gang has a tip-off about a wealthy farmer and a tax-collector travelling to London. Falstaff sees himself as youthful, fit and brave, but his behaviour in this episode does not match up to this image.

Prince Henry enjoys Falstaff's company, but he knows his faults. He sees him as a foolish man rather than as an evil man, because he refuses to act his age, and gets himself into worse trouble by trying to talk himself out of difficulties. Hal knows that being involved in robbing his own father's official could get him into trouble, but he sees a way of avoiding direct involvement and having some fun at the same time.

Falstaff is a comic character. He can be seen as a lovable old rogue or as a cheat and a liar. Later, in *Henry IV Part II*, Shakespeare shows the Prince breaking off his friendship with Falstaff and these rogues. However, he does not think he has wasted his time with them. He feels he has learned a lot about the ordinary people he must lead when he takes over from his father.

Script

Act II, Scene 1

Rochester. An inn yard

Enter a Carrier with a lantern in his hand

FIRST CARRIER:	Heigh-ho! an it be not four by the day, I'll be hanged: Charles' wain is over the new chimney, and yet our horse not packed. What, ostler!
OSTLER:	*(Within)* Anon, anon.
FIRST CARRIER:	I prithee, Tom, beat Cut's saddle, put a few flocks in the point; poor jade, is wrung in the withers out of all cess.

Enter another Carrier

SECOND CARRIER:	Peas and beans are as dank here as a dog, and that is the next way to give poor jades the bots: this house is turned upside down since Robin Ostler died.
FIRST CARRIER:	Poor fellow, never joyed since the price of oats rose; it was the death of him.
SECOND CARRIER:	I think this be the most villanous house in all London road for fleas: I am stung like a tench.
FIRST CARRIER:	Like a tench! by the mass, there is ne'er a king christen could be better bit than I have been since the first cock.
SECOND CARRIER:	Why, they will allow us ne'er a jordan, and then we leak in your chimney; and your chamber-lie breeds fleas like a loach.
FIRST CARRIER:	What, ostler! come away and be hanged!
SECOND CARRIER:	I have a gammon of bacon and two razes of ginger, to be delivered as far as Charing-cross.
FIRST CARRIER:	God's body! the turkeys in my pannier are quite starved. What, ostler! A plague on thee! hast thou never an eye in thy head? Canst not hear?

Enter Gadshill

GADSHILL:	Good morrow, carriers. What's o'clock?
FIRST CARRIER:	I think it be two o'clock.
GADSHILL:	I pray thee lend me thy lantern, to see my gelding in the stable.
FIRST CARRIER:	Nay, by God, soft; I know a trick worth two of that, i' faith.
GADSHILL:	I pray thee, lend me thine.
SECOND CARRIER:	Ay, when? can'st tell? Lend me thy lantern, quoth he? marry, I'll see thee hanged first.

GADSHILL:	Sirrah carrier, what time do you mean to come to London?
SECOND CARRIER:	Time enough to go to bed with a candle, I warrant thee. Come, neighbour Mugs, we'll call up the gentleman: they will along with company, for they have great charge.

Exeunt carriers

GADSHILL:	What, ho! chamberlain!

Enter Chamberlain

CHAMBERLAIN:	Good morrow, Master Gadshill. It holds current that I told you yesternight: there's a franklin in the wild of Kent hath brought three hundred marks with him in gold: I heard him tell it to one of his company last night at supper. They are up already, and call for eggs and butter; they will away presently.
GADSHILL:	Sirrah, if they meet not with Saint Nicholas' clerks, I'll give thee this neck.
CHAMBERLAIN:	No, I'll none of it: I pray thee keep that for the hangman; for I know thou worshippest Saint Nicholas as truly as a man of falsehood may.
GADSHILL:	What talkest thou to me of the hangman? if I hang, I'll make a fat pair of gallows; for if I hang, old Sir John hangs with me, and thou knowest he is no starveling. Tut! I am joined with no foot land-rakers, no long-staff sixpenny strikers, none of these mad mustachio purple-hued malt-worms; but with nobility and tranquillity, burgomasters and great oneyers, such as can hold in, such as will strike sooner than speak, and speak sooner than drink, and drink sooner than pray. Give me thy hand: thou shalt have a share in our purchase, as I am a true man. Bid the ostler bring my gelding out of the stable. Farewell, you muddy knave.

Exeunt

Act II, Scene 2

The highway

Enter Prince Henry and Poins

POINS:	Come, shelter, shelter: I have removed Falstaff's horse, and he frets like a gummed velvet.
PRINCE HENRY:	Stand close.

Enter Falstaff

FALSTAFF:	Poins! Poins, and be hanged! Poins!
PRINCE HENRY:	Peace, ye fat-kidneyed rascal! what a brawling dost thou keep!

FALSTAFF:	Where's Poins, Hal?
PRINCE HENRY:	He is walked up to the top of the hill: I'll go seek him.
FALSTAFF:	I am accursed to rob in that thief's company: the rascal hath removed my horse, and tied him I know not where. If I travel but four foot by the squier further afoot, I shall break my wind. Well, I doubt not but to die a fair death for all this, if I 'scape hanging for killing that rogue. I have forsworn his company hourly any time this two and twenty years, and yet I am bewitched with the rogue's company. If the rascal hath not given me medicines to make me love him, I'll be hanged; it could not be else: I have drunk medicines. Poins! Hal! a plague upon you both! Bardolph! Peto! I'll starve ere I'll rob a foot further. Eight yards of uneven ground is threescore and ten miles afoot with me; and the stony-hearted villains know it well enough: a plague upon it when thieves cannot be true one to another!

They whistle

	Whew! A plague upon you all! Give me my horse, you rogues; give me my horse, and be hanged!
PRINCE HENRY:	Peace, ye fat-guts! lie down; lay thine ear close to the ground and list if thou canst hear the tread of travellers.
FALSTAFF:	Have you any levers to lift me up again, being down? 'Sblood, I'll not bear mine own flesh so far afoot again for all the coin in thy father's exchequer. What a plague mean ye to colt me thus?
PRINCE HENRY:	Thou liest; thou art not colted, thou art uncolted.
FALSTAFF:	I prithee, good Prince Hal, help me to my horse, good king's son.
PRINCE HENRY:	Out, ye rogue! shall I be your ostler?
FALSTAFF:	Go, hang thyself in thine own heir-apparent garters! If I be ta'en, I'll peach for this. An I have not ballads made on you all and sung to filthy tunes, let a cup of sack be my poison: when a jest is so forward, and afoot too! I hate it.

Enter Gadshill, Bardolph and Peto

GADSHILL:	Stand.
FALSTAFF:	So I do, against my will.
POINS:	O, 'tis our setter: I know his voice.
BARDOLPH:	What news?
GADSHILL:	Case ye, case ye; on with your vizards: there's money of

	the king's coming down the hill; 'tis going to the king's exchequer.
FALSTAFF:	You lie, ye rogue; 'tis going to the king's tavern.
GADSHILL:	There's enough to make us all.
FALSTAFF:	To be hanged.
PRINCE HENRY:	Sirs, you four shall front them in the narrow lane; Ned Poins and I will walk lower: if they 'scape from your encounter, then they light on us.
PETO:	How many be there of them?
GADSHILL:	Some eight or ten.
FALSTAFF:	'Zounds, will they not rob us?
PRINCE HENRY:	What, a coward, Sir John Paunch?
FALSTAFF:	Indeed, I am not John of Gaunt, your grandfather; but yet no coward, Hal.
PRINCE HENRY:	Well, we leave that to the proof.
PETO:	Sirrah Jack, thy horse stands behind the hedge: when thou needest him, there thou shalt find him. Farewell, and stand fast.
FALSTAFF:	Now cannot I strike him, if I should be hanged.
PRINCE HENRY:	*(Aside to Poins)* Ned, where are our disguises?
PETO:	*(Aside to Prince)* Here, hard by: stand close.

Exeunt Prince Henry and Poins

FALSTAFF:	Now, my masters: every man to his business.

Enter the Travellers

FIRST TRAVELLER:	Come, neighbour: the boy shall lead our horses down the hill; we'll walk afoot awhile, and ease our legs.
THIEVES:	Stand!
TRAVELLERS:	Jesus bless us!
FALSTAFF:	Strike; down with them; cut the villains' throats: ah! whoreson caterpillars! bacon-fed knaves! They hate us youth: down with them: fleece them.
TRAVELLERS:	O, we are undone, both we and ours for ever!
FALSTAFF:	Hang ye, gorbellied knaves, are ye undone? No, ye fat chuffs: I would your store were here! On, bacons, on! What, ye knaves! young men must live. You are Grand-jurors, are ye? we'll jure ye, 'faith.

They rob them and bind them. Exeunt

Re-enter Prince Henry and Poins disguised

PRINCE HENRY:	The thieves have bound the true men. Now could thou and I rob the thieves, and go merrily to London, it

would be argument for a week, laughter for a month,
and a good jest for ever.

POINS: Stand close; I hear them coming.

They retire. Enter the Thieves again

FALSTAFF: Come, my masters, let us share, and then to horse before
day. An the Prince and Poins be not two arrant
cowards, there's no equity stirring: there's no more
valour in that Poins than in a wild-duck.

As they are sharing, the Prince and Poins set upon them

PRINCE HENRY: Your money!

POINS: Villains!

*They all run away; and Falstaff, after a blow or two, runs away too, leaving the
booty behind them*

PRINCE HENRY: Got with much ease. Now merrily to horse: the thieves
are all scatter'd and possess'd with fear so strongly that
they dare not meet each other; each takes his fellow for
an officer. Away, good Ned. Falstaff sweats to death,
and lards the lean earth as he walks along. Were 't not
for laughing, I should pity him.

POINS: How the fat rogue roar'd!

Exeunt

Act II, Scene 4

The Boar's-Head Tavern, Eastcheap

Enter Prince Henry

VINTNER: My lord, old Sir John, with half-a-dozen more, are at the
door: shall I let them in?

PRINCE HENRY: Let them alone awhile, and then open the door.

Exit Vintner

Poins!

Enter Poins

POINS: Anon, anon, sir.

PRINCE HENRY: Sirrah, Falstaff and the rest of the thieves are at the door:
shall we be merry?

POINS: As merry as crickets, my lad.

PRINCE HENRY: I prithee, call in Falstaff. Call in ribs, call in tallow.

Enter Falstaff, Gadshill, Bardolph, and Peto; Francis following with wine

POINS: Welcome, Jack: where hast thou been?

FALSTAFF: A plague of all cowards, I say, and a vengeance too!
marry, and amen! Give me a cup of sack, boy. Ere I

lead this life long, I'll sew nether stocks and mend
them and foot them too. A plague of all cowards!
Give me a cup of sack, rogue. Is there no virtue extant?
(He drinks) You rogue, here's lime in this sack too: there is nothing
but roguery to be found in villanous man: yet a
coward is worse than a cup of sack with lime in it. A
villanous coward! Go thy ways, old Jack; die when
thou wilt, if manhood, good manhood, be not forgot
upon the face of the earth, then am I a shotten herring.
There live not three good men unhanged in England;
and one of them is fat and grows old: God help the
while! a bad world, I say. I would I were a weaver; I
could sing psalms or any thing. A plague of all
cowards, I say still.

PRINCE HENRY: How now, wool-sack! what mutter you?

FALSTAFF: A king's son! If I do not beat thee out of thy kingdom
with a dagger of lath, and drive all thy subjects afore
thee like a flock of wild-geese, I'll never wear hair on
my face more. You Prince of Wales!

PRINCE HENRY: Why, you whoreson round man, what's the matter?

FALSTAFF: Are not you a coward? Answer me to that: and
Poins there?

POINS: 'Zounds, ye fat paunch, an ye call me coward, by the
Lord, I'll stab thee.

FALSTAFF: I call thee coward! I'll see thee damned ere I call thee
coward: but I would give a thousand pound I could
run as fast as thou canst. You are straight enough in
the shoulders, you care not who sees your back: call
you that backing of your friends? A plague upon such
backing! give me them that will face me. Give me a
cup of sack: I am a rogue, if I drunk to-day.

PRINCE HENRY: O villain! thy lips are scarce wiped since thou
drunkest last.

FALSTAFF: All's one for that. *(He drinks)* A plague of all cowards,
still say I.

PRINCE HENRY: What's the matter?

FALSTAFF: What's the matter! there be four of us here have ta'en a
thousand pound this day morning.

PRINCE HENRY: Where is it, Jack? where is it?

FALSTAFF: Where is it! taken from us it is: a hundred upon poor
four of us.

PRINCE HENRY: What, a hundred, man?

FALSTAFF: I am a rogue, if I were not at half-sword with a dozen of them two hours together. I have 'scaped by miracle. I am eight times thrust through the doublet, four through the hose; my buckler cut through and through; my sword hacked like a hand-saw – ecce signum! I never dealt better since I was a man: all would not do. A plague of all cowards! Let them speak: if they speak more or less than truth, they are villains and the sons of darkness.

PRINCE HENRY: Speak, sirs; how was it?

GADSHILL: We four set upon some dozen—

FALSTAFF: Sixteen at least, my lord.

GADSHILL: And bound them.

PETO: No, no, they were not bound.

FALSTAFF: You rogue, they were bound, every man of them; or I am a Jew else, an Ebrew Jew.

GADSHILL: As we were sharing, some six or seven fresh men set upon us—

FALSTAFF: And unbound the rest, and then come in the other.

PRINCE HENRY: What, fought you with them all?

FALSTAFF: All! I know not what you call all; but if I fought not with fifty of them, I am a bunch of radish: if there were not two or three and fifty upon poor old Jack, then am I no two-legged creature.

PRINCE HENRY: Pray God you have not murdered some of them.

FALSTAFF: Nay, that's past praying for: I have peppered two of them; two I am sure I have paid, two rogues in buckram suits. I tell thee what, Hal, if I tell thee a lie, spit in my face, call me horse. Thou knowest my old ward; here I lay and thus I bore my point. Four rogues in buckram let drive at me—

PRINCE HENRY: What, four? thou saidst but two even now.

FALSTAFF: Four, Hal; I told thee four.

POINS: Ay, ay, he said four.

FALSTAFF: These four came all a-front, and mainly thrust at me. I made me no more ado but took all their seven points in my target, thus.

PRINCE HENRY: Seven? why, there were but four even now.

FALSTAFF: In buckram?

POINS: Ay, four, in buckram suits.

FALSTAFF: Seven, by these hilts, or I am a villain else.

PRINCE HENRY: Prithee, let him alone; we shall have more anon.

FALSTAFF: Dost thou hear me, Hal?

PRINCE HENRY: Ay, and mark thee too, Jack.

FALSTAFF: Do so, for it is worth the listening to. These nine in buckram that I told thee of—

PRINCE HENRY: So, two more already.

FALSTAFF: Their points being broken,—

POINS: Down fell their hose.

FALSTAFF: Began to give me ground: but I followed me close, came in foot and hand; and with a thought seven of the eleven I paid.

PRINCE HENRY: O monstrous! eleven buckram men grown out of two!

FALSTAFF: But, as the devil would have it, three misbegotten knaves in Kendal green came at my back and let drive at me; for it was so dark, Hal, that thou couldst not see thy hand.

PRINCE HENRY: These lies are like their father that begets them; gross as a mountain, open, palpable. Why, thou clay-brained guts, thou knotty-pated fool, thou whoreson, obscene, grease tallow-catch,—

FALSTAFF: What, art thou mad? Art thou mad? Is not the truth the truth?

PRINCE HENRY: Why, how couldst thou know these men in Kendal green, when it was so dark thou couldst not see thy hand? Come, tell us your reason: what sayest thou to this?

POINS: Come, your reason, Jack, your reason.

FALSTAFF: What, upon compulsion? 'Zounds, an I were at the strappado, or all the racks in the world, I would not tell you on compulsion. Give you a reason on compulsion! If reasons were as plentiful as blackberries, I would give no man a reason upon compulsion, I.

PRINCE HENRY: I'll be no longer guilty of this sin; this sanguine coward, this bed-presser, this horseback-breaker, this huge hill of flesh,—

FALSTAFF: 'Sblood, you starveling, you eel-skin, you dried neat's tongue, you bull's pizzle, you stock-fish! O for breath to utter what is like thee! You tailor's-yard, you sheath, you bowcase; you vile standing-tuck,—

PRINCE HENRY: Well, breathe awhile, and then to it again: and when thou hast tired thyself in base comparisons, hear me speak but this.

POINS: Mark, Jack.

PRINCE HENRY: We two saw you four set on four and bound them, and were masters of their wealth. Mark now, how a plain tale shall put you down. Then did we two set on you four; and, with a word, out-faced you from your prize, and have it; yea, and can show it you here in the house: and, Falstaff, you carried your guts away as nimbly, with as quick dexterity, and roared for mercy and still run and roared, as ever I heard bull-calf. What a slave art thou, to hack thy sword as thou hast done, and then say it was in fight! What trick, what device, what starting-hole, canst thou now find out to hide thee from this open and apparent shame?

POINS: Come, let's hear, Jack; what trick hast thou now?

FALSTAFF: By the Lord, I knew ye as well as he that made ye. Why, hear you, my masters: was it for me to kill the heir-apparent? should I turn upon the true prince? why, thou knowest I am as valiant as Hercules: but beware instinct; the lion will not touch the true prince. Instinct is a great matter; I was now a coward on instinct. I shall think the better of myself, and thee, during my life – I for a valiant lion, and thou for a true prince. But, by the Lord, lads, I am glad you have the money. Hostess, clap to the doors: watch to-night, pray to-morrow. Gallants, lads, boys, hearts of gold, all the titles of good fellowship come to you! What, shall we be merry? shall we have a play extempore?

PRINCE HENRY: Content; and the argument shall be thy running away.

FALSTAFF: Ah, no more of that, Hal, an thou lovest me!

Postscript

Purpose
- to amuse and entertain
- to show how a famous English king prepared for his duty

Effects
- laughter at Falstaff
- insight into Prince Hal's two lives

Devices
- verbal irony
- dramatic irony
- language of abuse
- language of exaggeration
- action sequence (robbery, second robbery and acted fight)

Kenneth Branagh as Hamlet in modern dress, 1992.

Read aloud the last line emphasising the word "thieves" first, and then "true". How does a different emphasis affect this line?

2 Read aloud the lines "Strike; down with them (…) we'll jure ye, 'faith" emphasising Falstaff's fierce instructions.

Does he say these lines to the travellers or to his companions? How close does he get to the travellers?

3 Where should the Prince and Poins be when Falstaff says "There's no more valour in that Poins than in a wild-duck"?

4 Describe (or make a sketch of) the setting you would use if you were filming the scene in the inn where Falstaff puts on his show of fighting. Remember what he did to his clothes and his sword.

5 Design a theatre poster or video cover showing Falstaff acting out his part as a great fighter.

In groups

1 Hot seat

a Put Prince Hal in the hot seat and ask him questions about his relationship with Falstaff and what he thinks of him.

b Put Falstaff in the hot seat and ask him why he has been involved in stealing merchants' money and the king's revenue.

2 Tableau talkback

The group freezes in a tableau of the scene at the inn. The questioner walks around the figures in the tableau and asks what different characters think about the situation.

3 Perform the robbery, bringing out Falstaff's loud (but perhaps not very active) part in the event. How would he make sure he didn't get into any danger?

4 Improvise a scene in which someone recounts their own superb performance on the football field, or rescuing someone from an attack by a group of brutal thugs.

5 Perform the section in the tavern, bringing out:

- Falstaff's increasing exaggeration of his brave deeds
- Falstaff's actions to accompany his description
- the way Hal and Poins prompt him to more detail by their questions and by pretending to believe him.

Social, cultural and historical aspects

What does the opening scene tell us about:

- conditions in lodging houses in Shakespeare's day (see the glossary)
- transport and trade in Shakespeare's day
- the risks of talking and travelling in the course of business
- crime and punishment?

Falstaff the great lover – from *The Merry Wives of Windsor*

Introduction

Sir John Falstaff is an old rogue who has spent most of his life avoiding work and seeking pleasure. He is very fond of wine, women and the company of idle drinkers. He is a comic character because he refuses to act his age, and is always on the lookout for the next amusement or advantage. However, he takes too many risks and often gets himself into trouble, as he does in this episode.

Falstaff has run out of money. He has heard that Mistress Page has access to her rich husband's wealth, and that Mistress Ford is also known to have a free hand with her husband's wallet. To make doubly sure of getting his hands on some money, Falstaff decides to write a love letter to both of the ladies.

Falstaff first appeared in *Henry IV Part I* and then in *Henry IV Part II*, where he died after being rejected by Prince Hal. Audiences loved his pranks and rudeness, and Shakespeare wrote this play to bring him back on the stage.

This painting from 1904 shows famous actors of their day, Ellen Terry and Herbert Beerbohm Tree, performing in 'The Merry Wives of Windsor'.

Script

Act II, Scene 1

Before Page's house

Enter Mistress Page, with a letter

MISTRESS PAGE: What, have I 'scaped love-letters in the holiday-time of my beauty, and am I now a subject for them? Let me see,

Reads

'Ask me no reason why I love you; for though Love use Reason for his precisian, he admits him not for his counsellor. You are not young, no more am I; go to then, there's sympathy: you are merry, so am I; ha, ha! then there's more sympathy: you love sack, and so do I; would you desire better sympathy? Let it suffice thee, Mistress Page, – at the least, if the love of soldier can suffice – that I love thee. I will not say, pity me; 'tis not a soldier-like phrase: but I say, love me.
By me,
Thine own true knight,
By day or night,
Or any kind of light,
With all his might
For thee to fight, JOHN FALSTAFF'
What a Herod of Jewry is this! O wicked, wicked world! One that is well-nigh worn to pieces with age to show himself a young gallant! What an unweighed behaviour hath this Flemish drunkard picked – with the devil's name! – out of my conversation, that he dares in this manner assay me? Why, he hath not been thrice in my company! What should I say to him? I was then frugal of my mirth: Heaven forgive me! Why, I'll exhibit a bill in the parliament for the putting down of men. How shall I be revenged on him? for revenged I will be, as sure as his guts are made of puddings.

Enter Mistress Ford

MISTRESS FORD: Mistress Page! trust me, I was going to your house.

MISTRESS PAGE: And, trust me, I was coming to you. You look very ill.

MISTRESS FORD: Nay, I'll ne'er believe that; I have to show to the contrary.

MISTRESS PAGE: Faith, but you do, in my mind.

MISTRESS FORD: Well, I do then; yet I say I could show you to the contrary. O Mistress Page, give me some counsel!

MISTRESS PAGE: What's the matter, woman?

MISTRESS FORD:	O woman, if it were not for one trifling respect, I could come to such honour!
MISTRESS PAGE:	Hang the trifle, woman! take the honour. What is it? Dispense with trifles; what is it?
MISTRESS FORD:	If I would but go to hell for an eternal moment or so I could be knighted.
MISTRESS PAGE:	What? thou liest! Sir Alice Ford! These knights will hack; and so thou shouldst not alter the article of thy gentry.
MISTRESS FORD:	We burn daylight: here, read, read; perceive how I might be knighted. I shall think the worse of fat men, as long as I have an eye to make difference of men's liking: and yet he would not swear; praised women's modesty; and gave such orderly and well-behaved reproof to all uncomeliness, that I would have sworn his disposition would have gone to the truth of his words; but they do no more adhere and keep place together than the Hundredth Psalm to the tune of 'Green Sleeves'. What tempest, I trow, threw this whale, with so many tuns of oil in his belly, ashore at Windsor? How shall I be revenged on him? I think the best way were to entertain him with hope, till the wicked fire of lust have melted him in his own grease. Did you ever hear the like?
MISTRESS PAGE:	Letter for letter, but that the name of Page and Ford differs! To thy great comfort in this mystery of ill opinions, here's the twin-brother of thy letter: but let thine inherit first; for, I protest, mine never shall. I warrant he hath a thousand of these letters, writ with blank space for different names – sure, more, – and these are of the second edition: he will print them, out of doubt; for he cares not what he puts into the press, when he would put us two. I had rather be a giantess, and lie under Mount Pelion. Well, I will find you twenty lascivious turtles ere one chaste man.
MISTRESS FORD:	Why, this is the very same; the very hand, the very words. What doth he think of us?
MISTRESS PAGE:	Nay, I know not: it makes me almost ready to wrangle with mine own honesty. I'll entertain myself like one that I am not acquainted withal; for, sure, unless he know some strain in me, that I know not myself, he would never have boarded me in this fury.
MISTRESS FORD:	'Boarding,' call you it? I'll be sure to keep him above deck.
MISTRESS PAGE:	So will I: if he come under my hatches, I'll never to sea again. Let's be revenged on him: let's appoint him a

meeting; give him a show of comfort in his suit and lead him on with a fine-baited delay, till he hath pawned his horses to mine host of the Garter.

MISTRESS FORD: Nay, I will consent to act any villainy against him, that may not sully the chariness of our honesty. O, that my husband saw this letter! It would give eternal food to his jealousy.

MISTRESS PAGE: Why, look where he comes; and my good man too: he's as far from jealousy as I am from giving him cause; and that I hope is an unmeasurable distance.

MISTRESS FORD: You are the happier woman.

MISTRESS PAGE: Let's consult together against this greasy knight. Come hither.

They retire

Act II, Scene 2

A room in the Garter Inn

FALSTAFF: I will not lend thee a penny.

PISTOL: Why, then the world's mine oyster. Which I with sword will open.

FALSTAFF: Not a penny. I have been content, sir, you should lay my countenance to pawn; I have grated upon my good friends for three reprieves for you and your coach-fellow Nym; or else you had looked through the grate, like a geminy of baboons. I am damned in hell for swearing to gentlemen my friends, you were good soldiers and tall fellows; and when Mistress Bridget lost the handle of her fan, I took't upon mine honour thou hadst it not.

PISTOL: Didst not thou share? hadst thou not fifteen pence?

FALSTAFF: Reason, you rogue, reason: thinkest thou I'll endanger my soul gratis? At a word, hang no more about me, I am no gibbet for you. Go. A short knife and a throng! To your manor of Pickt-hatch! Go. You'll not bear a letter for me, you rogue! You stand upon your honour! Why, thou unconfinable baseness, it is as much as I can do to keep the terms of my honour precise: I, I, I myself sometimes, leaving the fear of God on the left hand and hiding mine honour in my necessity, am fain to shuffle, to hedge and to lurch; and yet you, rogue, will ensconce your rags, your cat-a-mountain looks, your red-lattice phrases, and your bold-beating oaths, under the shelter of your honour! You will not do it, you!

PISTOL: I do relent: what would thou more of man?

Enter Robin

ROBIN:	Sir, here's a woman would speak with you.
FALSTAFF:	Let her approach.

Enter Mistress Quickly

MISTRESS QUICKLY:	Give your worship good morrow.
FALSTAFF:	Good morrow, good wife.
MISTRESS QUICKLY:	Not so, an't please your worship.
FALSTAFF:	Good maid, then.
MISTRESS QUICKLY:	I'll be sworn, as my mother was, the first hour I was born.
FALSTAFF:	I do believe the swearer. What with me?
MISTRESS QUICKLY:	Shall I vouchsafe your worship a word or two?
FALSTAFF:	Two thousand, fair woman: and I'll vouchsafe thee the hearing.
MISTRESS QUICKLY:	There is one Mistress Ford, sir: – I pray, come a little nearer this ways – I myself dwell with master Doctor Caius,—
FALSTAFF:	Well, on: Mistress Ford, you say,—
MISTRESS QUICKLY:	Your worship says very true: I pray your worship, come a little nearer this ways.
FALSTAFF:	I warrant thee, nobody hears; mine own people, mine own people.
MISTRESS QUICKLY:	Are they so? God bless them and make them his servants!
FALSTAFF:	Well, Mistress Ford; what of her?
MISTRESS QUICKLY:	Why, sir, she's a good creature. Lord Lord! Your worship's a wanton! Well, heaven forgive you and all of us, I pray!
FALSTAFF:	Mistress Ford; come, Mistress Ford,—
MISTRESS QUICKLY:	Marry, this is the short and the long of it; you have brought her into such a canaries as 'tis wonderful. The best courtier of them all, when the court lay at Windsor, could never have brought her to such a canary. Yet there has been knights, and lords, and gentlemen, with their coaches, I warrant you, coach after coach, letter after letter, gift after gift; smelling so sweetly, all musk, and so rushling, I warrant you, in silk and gold; and in such alligant terms; and in such wine and sugar of the best and the fairest, that would have won any woman's heart; and, I warrant you, they could never get an eye-wink of her: I had myself twenty angels given me this morning; but I defy all angels, in any such sort, as they say, but in the way of honesty: and, I warrant you, they

could never get her so much as sip on a cup with the proudest of them all: and yet there has been earls, nay, which is more, pensioners; but, I warrant you, all is one with her.

FALSTAFF: But what says she to me? be brief, my good she-Mercury.

MISTRESS QUICKLY: Marry, she hath received your letter, for the which she thanks you a thousand times; and she gives you to notify that her husband will be absence from his house between ten and eleven.

FALSTAFF: Ten and eleven?

MISTRESS QUICKLY: Ay, forsooth; and then you may come and see the picture, she says, that you wot of: Master Ford, her husband, will be from home. Alas! the sweet woman leads an ill life with him: he's a very jealousy man: she leads a very frampold life with him, good heart.

FALSTAFF: Ten and eleven. Woman, commend me to her; I will not fail her.

MISTRESS QUICKLY: Why, you say well. But I have another messenger to your worship. Mistress Page hath her hearty commendations to you too: and let me tell you in your ear, she's as fartuous a civil modest wife, and one, I tell you, that will not miss you morning nor evening prayer, as any is in Windsor, whoe'er be the other: and she bade me tell your worship that her husband is seldom from home; but she hopes there will come a time. I never knew a woman so dote upon a man: surely I think you have charms, la; yes, in truth.

FALSTAFF: Not I, I assure thee: setting the attractions of my good parts aside I have no other charms.

MISTRESS QUICKLY: Blessing on your heart for't!

FALSTAFF: But, I pray thee, tell me this: has Ford's wife and Page's wife acquainted each other how they love me?

MISTRESS QUICKLY: That were a jest indeed! they have not so little grace, I hope: that were a trick indeed! But Mistress Page would desire you to send her your little page, of all loves: her husband has a marvellous infection to the little page; and truly Master Page is an honest man. Never a wife in Windsor leads a better life than she does: do what she will, say what she will, take all, pay all, go to bed when she list, rise when she list, all is as she will: and truly she deserves it; for if there be a kind woman in Windsor, she is one. You must send her your page; no remedy.

FALSTAFF:	Why, I will.
MISTRESS QUICKLY:	Nay, but do so, then: and, look you, he may come and go between you both; and in any case have a nay-word, that you may know one another's mind, and the boy never need to understand any thing; for 'tis not good that children should know any wickedness: old folks, you know, have discretion, as they say, and know the world.
FALSTAFF:	Fare thee well: commend me to them both: there's my purse; I am yet thy debtor. Boy, go along with this woman.

Exeunt Mistress Quickly and Robin

This news distracts me!

Act III, Scene 3

A room in Ford's house

Enter Mistress Ford and Mistress Page

MISTRESS FORD:	What, John! What, Robert!
MISTRESS PAGE:	Quickly, quickly! is the buck-basket—
MISTRESS FORD:	I warrant. What, Robin, I say!

Enter Servants with a basket

MISTRESS PAGE:	Come, come, come.
MISTRESS FORD:	Here, set it down.
MISTRESS PAGE:	Give your men the charge; we must be brief.
MISTRESS FORD:	Marry, as I told you before, John and Robert, be ready here hard by in the brew-house: and when I suddenly call you, come forth, and without any pause or staggering take this basket on your shoulders; that done, trudge with it in all haste, and carry it among the whitsters in Datchet-mead, and there empty it in the muddy ditch close by the Thames side.
MISTRESS PAGE:	You will do it?
MISTRESS FORD:	I ha' told them over and over; they lack no direction. Be gone, and come when you are called.

Exeunt Servants

MISTRESS PAGE:	Here comes little Robin.

Enter Robin

MISTRESS FORD:	How now, my eyas-musket! what news with you?
ROBIN:	My master, Sir John, is come in at your back-door, Mistress Ford, and requests your company.
MISTRESS PAGE:	You little Jack-a-Lent, have you been true to us?

ROBIN: Ay, I'll be sworn. My master knows not of your being here and hath threatened to put me into everlasting liberty if I tell you of it; for he swears he'll turn me away.

MISTRESS PAGE: Thou'rt a good boy: this secrecy of thine shall be a tailor to thee and shall make thee a new doublet and hose. I'll go hide me.

MISTRESS FORD: Do so. Go tell thy master I am alone.

Exit Robin

Mistress Page, remember you your cue.

MISTRESS PAGE: I warrant thee; if I do not act it, hiss me.

Exit

MISTRESS FORD: Go to, then; we'll use this unwholesome humidity, this gross watery pumpion; we'll teach him to know turtles from jays.

Enter Falstaff

FALSTAFF: Have I caught thee, my heavenly jewel? Why, now let me die, for I have lived long enough: this is the period of my ambition: O this blessed hour!

MISTRESS FORD: O sweet Sir John!

FALSTAFF: Mistress Ford, I cannot cog, I cannot prate, Mistress Ford. Now shall I sin in my wish: I would thy husband were dead: I'll speak it before the best lord; I would make thee my lady.

MISTRESS FORD: I your lady, Sir John! alas, I should be a pitiful lady!

FALSTAFF: Let the court of France show me such another. I see how thine eye would emulate the diamond: thou hast the right arched beauty of the brow that becomes the ship-tire, the tire-valiant, or any tire of Venetian admittance.

MISTRESS FORD: A plain kerchief, Sir John: my brows become nothing else; nor that well neither.

FALSTAFF: By the Lord, thou art a tyrant to say so: thou wouldst make an absolute courtier; and the firm fixture of thy foot would give an excellent motion to thy gait in a semicircled farthingale. I see what thou wert, if Fortune thy foe were not, Nature thy friend. Come, thou canst not hide it.

MISTRESS FORD: Believe me, there is no such thing in me.

FALSTAFF: What made me love thee? let that persuade thee there's something extraordinary in thee. Come, I cannot cog and say thou art this and that, like a many of these lisping hawthorn-buds, that come like women in men's apparel, and smell like Bucklersbury in simple time; I cannot: but I love thee; none but thee; and thou deservest it.

MISTRESS FORD: Do not betray me, sir. I fear you love Mistress Page.

FALSTAFF: Thou mightst as well say I love to walk by the Counter-gate, which is as hateful to me as the reek of a lime-kiln.

MISTRESS FORD: Well, heaven knows how I love you; and you shall one day find it.

FALSTAFF: Keep in that mind; I'll deserve it.

MISTRESS FORD: Nay, I must tell you, so you do; or else I could not be in that mind.

ROBIN: *Within* Mistress Ford, Mistress Ford! here's Mistress Page at the door, sweating and blowing and looking wildly, and would needs speak with you presently.

FALSTAFF: She shall not see me: I will ensconce me behind the arras.

MISTRESS FORD: Pray you, do so: she's a very tattling woman.

Falstaff hides himself

Re-enter Mistress Page and Robin

What's the matter? how now!

MISTRESS PAGE: O Mistress Ford, what have you done? You're shamed, you're overthrown, you're undone for ever!

MISTRESS FORD: What's the matter, good Mistress Page?

MISTRESS PAGE: O well-a-day, Mistress Ford! having an honest man to your husband, to give him such cause of suspicion!

MISTRESS FORD: What cause of suspicion?

MISTRESS PAGE: What cause of suspicion! Out upon you! how am I mistook in you!

MISTRESS FORD: Why, alas, what's the matter?

MISTRESS PAGE: Your husband's coming hither, woman, with all the officers in Windsor, to search for a gentleman that he says is here now in the house by your consent, to take an ill advantage of his absence: you are undone.

MISTRESS FORD: 'Tis not so, I hope.

MISTRESS PAGE: Pray heaven it be not so, that you have such a man here! but 'tis most certain your husband's coming, with half Windsor at his heels, to search for such a one. I come before to tell you. If you know yourself clear, why, I am glad of it; but if you have a friend here convey, convey him out. Be not amazed; call all your

	senses to you; defend your reputation, or bid farewell to your good life for ever.
MISTRESS FORD:	What shall I do? There is a gentleman my dear friend; and I fear not mine own shame so much as his peril: I had rather than a thousand pound he were out of the house.
MISTRESS PAGE:	For shame! never stand 'you had rather' and 'you had rather': your husband's here at hand, bethink you of some conveyance: in the house you cannot hide him. O, how have you deceived me! Look, here is a basket: if he be of any reasonable stature, he may creep in here; and throw foul linen upon him, as if it were going to bucking: or – it is whiting-time – send him by your two men to Datchet-mead.
MISTRESS FORD:	He's too big to go in there. What shall I do?
FALSTAFF:	*Coming forward* Let me see't, let me see't, O, let me see't! I'll in, I'll in. Follow your friend's counsel. I'll in.
MISTRESS PAGE:	What, Sir John Falstaff! Are these your letters, knight?
FALSTAFF:	I love thee. Help me away. Let me creep in here. I'll never—

Gets into the basket; they cover him with foul linen

MISTRESS PAGE:	Help to cover your master, boy. Call your men, Mistress Ford. You dissembling knight!
MISTRESS FORD:	What, John! Robert! John!

Exit Robin

Re-enter Servants

	Go take up these clothes here quickly. Where's the cowl-staff? look, how you drumble! Carry them to the laundress in Datchet-mead; quickly, come.

Enter Ford, Page, Doctor Caius, and Sir Hugh Evans

FORD:	Pray you, come near: if I suspect without cause, why then make sport at me; then let me be your jest; I deserve it. How now! whither bear you this?
SERVANT:	To the laundress, forsooth.
MISTRESS FORD:	Why, what have you to do whither they bear it? You were best meddle with buck-washing.
FORD:	Buck! I would I could wash myself of the buck! Buck, buck, buck! Ay, buck; I warrant you, buck; and of the season too, it shall appear.

Exeunt Servants with the basket

This painting from 1757 shows a performance of 'Hamlet'.

Postscript

Purpose
- to entertain and amuse

Effects
- laughter at Falstaff's deserved downfall
- laughter at the two women's contrasted response to the letter

Devices
- anticipation of events (instructions to servants about the basket)
- dramatic irony (use of arras)
- slapstick/farce in use of basket and foul linen
- parody of language of romance in letter and speech

Glossary

precisian	accurate measure like a Puritan
counsellor	trusted friend
sympathy	something in common
Herod of Jewry	evil man
gallant	fashionable ladies' man
Flemish	Flemish people were regarded as drunkards
assay	test, try out
frugal	sparing, ungenerous
liking	physical qualities
uncomeliness	improper behaviour
trow	wonder
Mount Pelion	one of the mountains under which the Titans were buried
lascivious	lustful, always thinking about sex
turtles	turtle-doves were thought to be faithful
chaste	pure and decent
entertain	amuse and think of
strain	tendency
boarded	got close to
suit	attempt to win affection
sully the chariness	blemish the integrity
countenance	good name, reputation
looked through the grate	been put in a prison cell
geminy	pair (gemini)
gratis	free
gibbet	frame for hanging executed corpses
red-lattice	ale-house (taverns had red-lattice windows)
canaries	Mistress Quickly's attempt at 'quandary'
musk	perfume
rushling	rustling
alligant	her attempt at 'elegant' (or 'eloquent')
angels	gold coins
Mercury	the swift bringer of messages to the gods

wot	know
frampold	bad-tempered
fartuous	her attempt at 'virtuous'
charms	magic potions
list	chooses
nay-word	password
buck-basket	washing-basket
whitsters in Datchet-Mead	linen-bleachers in the meadows near the Thames
eyas-musket	young male sparrow-hawk
Jack-a-Lent	brightly coloured dummy
pumpion	pumpkin
cog	lie
prate	speak at length
ship-tire	headdress like a ship's sails
tire-valiant	very ornamental headdress
Venetian	Venice was regarded as a place of great fashion
farthingale	petticoat stretched over hoops
hawthorn-buds	young spring-time growths
Bucklersbury	London market street where herbs were sold
simple time	summer (when herbs grow)
Counter-gate	a foul-smelling prison in London
lime-kiln	place where lime is manufactured, producing an unpleasant smell
arras	a thick hanging curtain on the wall
bucking	washing
whiting-time	time for bleaching linen
cowl-staff	pole used for carrying a tub (through its handles)
drumble	move slowly

Close-up on language

1 Which words does Mistress Page use to show her contempt for Falstaff?

2 Which words of Falstaff's show that he thinks he is better than Pistol?

3 Which words show that Mistress Quickly makes mistakes in her use of words?

Understanding character

Getting into thoughts and feelings

When Mistress Ford says "What tempest, I trow, threw this whale, with so many tuns of oil in his belly, ashore at Windsor?", she feels disgusted with Falstaff, and thinks he is gross and unattractive. On the other hand, before she heard Mistress Page's opinion, she wanted advice on whether to accept Falstaff's offer and may have been tempted: 'I could come to such honour!" For a moment she thought that being the partner of Sir John Falstaff could be an advantage.

1 Falstaff's letter tries to persuade Mistress Page that she has a lot in common with him, and should welcome his advances. He thinks she will be impressed with his claim that they are both old and therefore well suited. Think about her response to this letter, and how flattering she finds it.

2 What is Mistress Page thinking and feeling at these points?

"One that is well-nigh worn to pieces with age to show himself a young gallant!"
"Why, he hath not been thrice in my company (...) I was then frugal of my mirth"
"I'll exhibit a bill in the parliament for the putting down of men"
"I will find you twenty lascivious turtles ere one chaste man"

3 What is Mistress Ford thinking and feeling at these points?

"if it were not for one trifling respect, I could come to such honour!"
"I'll be sure to keep him above deck."
"It would give eternal food to his jealousy."

4 What is Falstaff's attitude to Pistol at this point?

"Not a penny. I have been content, sir, you should lay my countenance to pawn..."

5 What does Falstaff feel about Mistress Quickly at this point?

"But what says she to me? be brief, my good she-Mercury."

6 What attitude is Falstaff taking at this point?

"Not I, I assure thee: setting the attractions of my good parts
aside I have no other charms."

Personal response

1 The women see Falstaff's dishonest behaviour as typical of men. Do you think this is true?

2 If you found that someone had sent identical love letters to you and your best friend would you be:

- amused but not interested
- flattered and keen to write back before your friend
- insulted and speechless in disbelief
- insulted and determined to get your own back?

Or would you feel a mixture of these reactions?

Understanding performance

Staging and directing

1 What should the actor playing Mistress Page do at this point?

"Letter for letter, but that the name of Page and Ford differs!"

2 What should the actor playing Mistress Ford do at this point?

"What doth he think of us?"

3 What could costume and props add to the effect of the scene at the Garter Inn? Think about:

- Falstaff's clothes
- what he may be holding
- Pistol's clothes.

Practical work

Solo or in pairs

1 Read the line "What doth he think of us?" using a tone of:

- uncertain questioning
- angry disgust.

Which is better?

Does the line change its meaning if emphasis is put on "What" or "doth" or "think" or "us"?

2 Read the line "O, that my husband saw this letter! It would give eternal food to his jealousy" as if:

- she is afraid to make him jealous
- she would like to make him jealous.

Which do you think is better?

3 Describe (or make a sketch of) the setting you would use if you were filming the scene in Mistress Ford's house. Remember that Mistress Page needs to be hidden from Falstaff but visible to the audience.

4 Design a theatre poster or video cover showing Falstaff being tipped into the ditch.

In groups

1 **Hot seat**

a Put Mistress Page in the hot seat and question her about her feelings when she got the letter and when Falstaff came round to her house.

b Put Falstaff in the hot seat and question him about his disgraceful behaviour.

2 **Tableau talkback**

The group freezes in a tableau of the scene at Mistress Ford's. The questioner walks around the figures in the tableau and asks what different characters think about the situation.

3 Perform the wooing scene in Mistress Ford's house, bringing out:

- the feelings of Mistress Page and Mistress Ford
- Falstaff's attempt to charm, and then his panic
- both women's revenge as he gets into the basket.

Social, cultural and historical aspects

1 Does this episode seem familiar or unfamiliar to a modern audience? Look at each of the following:

- language
- characters
- comic situation
- attitudes of men
- attitudes of women.

Setting the trap – from *Much Ado About Nothing*

Introduction

Benedick is a young man who enjoys his freedom and doesn't want to settle down to marriage. He thinks romantic feelings are a sign of brain softening. He has a low opinion of Beatrice because she laughs at him and he does not always get the last word in their exchange of comments.

Beatrice is an independent woman who regards most of the women around her as too passive and too willing to please men. She considers most of the men she knows to be inferior to her in intelligence.

The friends of Beatrice and Benedick think they would make a very fine couple, but they know that they are both too proud to admit that they have anything in common.

In this extract from the play, Benedick changes his attitude. He starts by laughing at men who are stupid enough to fall in love with women, and ends by falling in love with Beatrice. This is because Don Pedro and Claudio and Leonato play a trick on him. They know he is hiding, so they pretend not to see him, and talk about how Beatrice is madly in love with him.

'Much Ado about Nothing' performed in modern dress by the Royal Shakespeare Company in 1993. Seen here are Mark Rylance and Janet McTeer.

Script

Act II, Scene 3

Leonato's orchard

Enter Benedick

BENEDICK: I do much wonder that one man, seeing how much another man is a fool when he dedicates his behaviours to love, will, after he hath laughed at such shallow follies in others, become the argument of his own scorn by falling in love: and such a man is Claudio.

I have known when there was no music with him but the drum and the fife; and now had he had rather hear the tabour and the pipe: I have known when he would have walked ten mile a-foot to see a good armour; and now will he lie ten nights awake, carving the fashion of a new doublet. He was wont to speak plain and to the purpose, like an honest man and a soldier; and now is he turned orthography; his words are a very fantastical banquet, just so many strange dishes. May I be so converted and see with these eyes? I cannot tell; I think not. Ha! the prince and Monsieur Love! I will hide me in the arbour.

Withdraws

Enter Don Pedro, Claudio, and Leonato

DON PEDRO: Come, shall we hear this music?

CLAUDIO: Yea, my good lord. How still the evening is, as hush'd on purpose to grace harmony!

DON PEDRO: See you where Benedick hath hid himself?

CLAUDIO: O, very well, my lord.

DON PEDRO: Come hither, Leonato. What was it you told me of today, that your niece Beatrice was in love with Signior Benedick?

CLAUDIO: O, ay: stalk on, stalk on; the fowl sits. I did never think that lady would have loved any man.

LEONATO: No, nor I neither; but most wonderful that she should so dote on Signior Benedick, whom she hath in all outward behaviours seemed ever to abhor.

BENEDICK: Is't possible? Sits the wind in that corner?

LEONATO: By my troth, my lord, I cannot tell what to think of it but that she loves him with an enraged affection: it is past the infinite of thought.

DON PEDRO: May be she doth but counterfeit.

CLAUDIO: Faith, like enough.

LEONATO: O God, counterfeit! There was never counterfeit of passion came so near the life of passion as she discovers it.

DON PEDRO: Why, what effects of passion shows she?

CLAUDIO: Bait the hook well; this fish will bite.

LEONATO: What effects, my lord? She will sit you, you heard my daughter tell you how.

CLAUDIO: She did, indeed.

DON PEDRO: How, how, I pray you? You amaze me: I would have thought her spirit had been invincible against all assaults of affection.

LEONATO: I would have sworn it had, my lord; especially against Benedick.

BENEDICK: I should think this a gull, but that the white-bearded fellow speaks it: knavery cannot, sure, hide himself in such reverence.

CLAUDIO: He hath ta'en the infection: hold it up.

DON PEDRO: Hath she made her affection known to Benedick?

LEONATO: No; and swears she never will: that's her torment.

CLAUDIO: 'Tis true, indeed; so your daughter says: 'Shall I,' says she, 'that have so oft encountered him with scorn, write to him that I love him?'

LEONATO: This says she now when she is beginning to write to him; for she'll be up twenty times a night, and there will she sit in her smock till she have writ a sheet of paper: my daughter tells us all.

CLAUDIO: Now you talk of a sheet of paper, I remember a pretty jest your daughter told us of.

LEONATO: O, when she had writ it and was reading it over, she found Benedick and Beatrice between the sheet?

CLAUDIO: That.

LEONATO: O, she tore the letter into a thousand halfpence; railed at herself, that she should be so immodest to write to one that she knew would flout her; 'I measure him,' says she, 'by my own spirit; for I should flout him, if he writ to me; yea, though I love him, I should.'

CLAUDIO: Then down upon her knees she falls, weeps, sobs, beats her heart, tears her hair, prays, curses; 'O sweet Benedick! God give me patience!'

LEONATO:	She doth indeed; my daughter says so: and the ecstasy hath so much overborne her that my daughter is sometime afeared she will do a desperate outrage to herself: it is very true.
DON PEDRO:	It were good that Benedick knew of it by some other, if she will not discover it.
CLAUDIO:	To what end? He would make but a sport of it and torment the poor lady worse.
DON PEDRO:	An he should, it were an alms to hang him. She's an excellent sweet lady; and, out of all suspicion, she is virtuous.
CLAUDIO:	And she is exceeding wise.
DON PEDRO:	In every thing but in loving Benedick.
LEONATO:	O, my lord, wisdom and blood combating in so tender a body, we have ten proofs to one that blood hath the victory. I am sorry for her, as I have just cause, being her uncle and her guardian.
DON PEDRO:	I would she had bestowed this dotage on me: I would have daffed all other respects and made her half myself. I pray you, tell Benedick of it, and hear what a' will say.
LEONATO:	Were it good, think you?
CLAUDIO:	Hero thinks surely she will die; for she says she will die, if he love her not, and she will die, ere she make her love known, and she will die, if he woo her, rather than she will bate one breath of her accustomed crossness.
DON PEDRO:	She doth well: if she should make tender of her love, 'tis very possible he'll scorn it; for the man, as you know all, hath a contemptible spirit.
CLAUDIO:	He is a very proper man.
DON PEDRO:	He hath indeed a good outward happiness.
CLAUDIO:	Before God! and, in my mind, very wise.
DON PEDRO:	He doth indeed show some sparks that are like wit.
CLAUDIO:	And I take him to be valiant.
DON PEDRO:	As Hector, I assure you: and in the managing of quarrels you may say he is wise; for either he avoids them with great discretion, or undertakes them with a most Christian-like fear.
LEONATO:	If he do fear God, a' must necessarily keep peace: if he break the peace, he ought to enter into a quarrel with fear and trembling.
DON PEDRO:	And so will he do; for the man doth fear God, howsoever it seems not in him by some large jests he

will make. Well I am sorry for your niece. Shall we go
seek Benedick, and tell him of her love?

CLAUDIO: Never tell him, my lord: let her wear it out with
good counsel.

LEONATO: Nay, that's impossible: she may wear her heart out first.

DON PEDRO: Well, we will hear further of it by your daughter: let it
cool the while. I love Benedick well; and I could wish he
would modestly examine himself, to see how much he is
unworthy so good a lady.

LEONATO: My lord, will you walk? dinner is ready.

CLAUDIO: If he do not dote on her upon this, I will never trust my
expectation.

DON PEDRO: Let there be the same net spread for her; and that must
your daughter and her gentlewomen carry. The sport
will be, when they hold one an opinion of another's
dotage, and no such matter: that's the scene that I would
see, which will be merely a dumb-show. Let us send her
to call him in to dinner.

Exeunt Don Pedro, Claudio, and Leonato

BENEDICK: *(Coming forward)* This can be no trick: the conference
was sadly borne. They have the truth of this from Hero.
They seem to pity the lady: it seems her affections have
their full bent. Love me! why, it must be requited. I hear
how I am censured: they say I will bear myself proudly,
if I perceive the love come from her; they say too that
she will rather die than give any sign of affection. I did
never think to marry: I must not seem proud: happy are
they that hear their detractions and can put them to
mending. They say the lady is fair – 'tis a truth, I can
bear them witness; and virtuous – 'tis so, I cannot
reprove it; and wise, but for loving me – by my troth, it
is no addition to her wit, nor no great argument of her
folly, for I will be horribly in love with her. I may chance
have some odd quirks and remnants of wit broken on
me, because I have railed so long against marriage: but
doth not the appetite alter? A man loves the meat in his
youth that he cannot endure in his age. Shall quips and
sentences and these paper bullets of the brain awe a man
from the career of his humour? No, the world must be
peopled. When I said I would die a bachelor, I did not
think I should live till I were married. Here comes
Beatrice. By this day she's a fair lady: I do spy some
marks of love in her.

Enter Beatrice

BEATRICE: Against my will I am sent to bid you come in to dinner.

BENEDICK: Fair Beatrice, I thank you for your pains.

BEATRICE: I took no more pains for those thanks than you take pains to thank me: if it had been painful, I would not have come.

BENEDICK: You take pleasure then in the message?

BEATRICE: Yea, just so much as you may take upon a knife's point and choke a daw withal. You have no stomach, signior: fare you well.

Exit

BENEDICK: Ha! 'Against my will I am sent to bid you come in to dinner': there's a double meaning in that. 'I took no more pains for those thanks than you took pains to thank me': that's as much as to say, Any pains that I take for you is easy as thanks. If I do not take pity of her, I am a villain; if I do not love her, I am a Jew. I will go get her picture.

Postscript

Purpose
- to entertain and amuse

Effects
- laughter at Benedick

Devices
- verbal irony
- dramatic irony
- concealment

Glossary

drum and *fife*	military musical instruments for marching
tabour and *pipe*	musical instruments to accompany dancing
doublet	upper garment like a waistcoat
was wont to	was disposed to
arbour	an ornamental hedge
the fowl sits	term from hunting birds: he's an easy target
she doth but	she only
counterfeit	put on a false show
gull	trick, deception
dotage	getting soft in the head for love
bate	stop
dumb-show	a mime

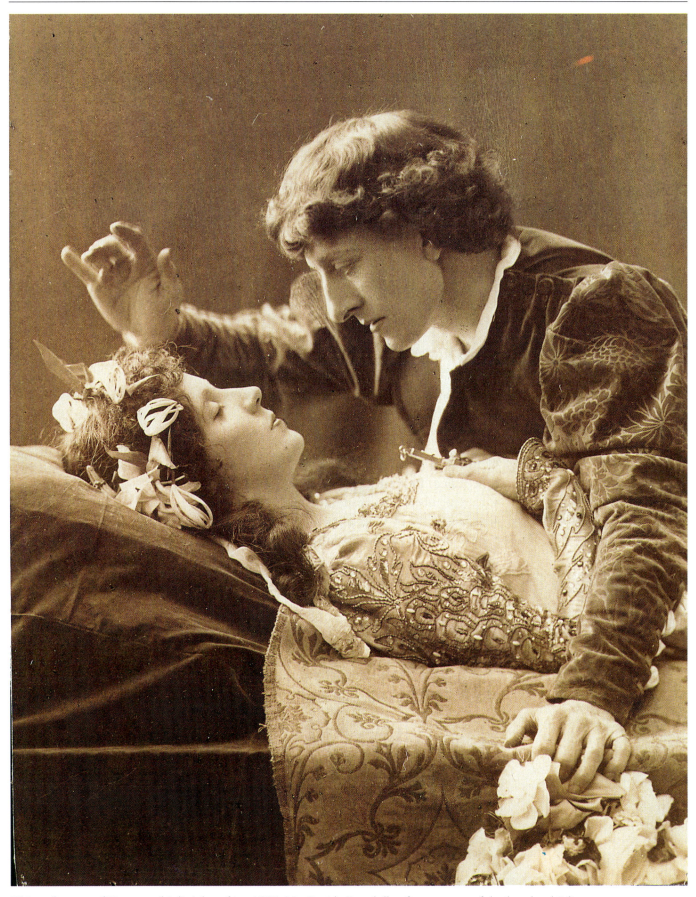

This performance of 'Romeo and Juliet' dates from 1895. Mrs Patrick Campbell, a famous actress of the day, played Juliet.

Close-up on language

1 Which words would a modern audience find unfamiliar?

2 Which unusual or unfamiliar words will make sense left as they are?

Understanding character

Getting into thoughts and feelings

Try to get inside a character's mind. Look at moments where the character reacts to a situation or to someone else and see what the character may be thinking or feeling at that moment.

When Benedick says "This can be no trick: the conference was sadly borne", what he says is what he feels. On the other hand, when he says "the world must be peopled" he is not really thinking of a duty to the human race. Rather he is feeling pleased that Beatrice finds him attractive, but he doesn't want to express such a soft-hearted sentiment.

1 Benedick laughs at his friend Claudio because falling in love has changed him. Why does he think it surprising that Claudio has changed?

Claudio used to like military music and soldiers' armour and he used to speak simply and plainly. How has he changed?

2 Benedick seems certain that he won't go the same way as Claudio. What makes him change?

- he realises Beatrice is the right person for him
- he remembers how beautiful she is
- he is flattered by what he hears
- he is annoyed that his friends say that he is not worth her love

3 What is Benedick thinking and feeling at these points?

> "and such a man is Claudio"
>
> "Sits the wind in that corner?"
>
> "They seem to pity the lady"
>
> "Fair Beatrice, I thank you for your pains."
>
> "there's a double meaning in that"

4 What is Claudio thinking and feeling at this point?

> "He hath ta'en the infection: hold it up."

Personal response

1 What impression do you get of Benedick from his first speech?

2 What impression do you get of him from his last speech?

3 If you had been part of the plot with Don Pedro, what would you have been tempted to say so that Benedick overheard it but was unable to answer?

Understanding performance

Staging and directing

1 The scene is set in an orchard, and the audience needs to see Benedick and his reactions as things are said about him.

a How can this be done? Think about using:

- a wall
- a hedge
- a tree.

b Where should Benedick be on the stage?

- with his back to the audience
- side on to the audience
- facing the audience from the back of the stage

c Could there be other ways of making it amusing? Consider using:

- a table
- a tool-shed
- a large barrel.

d What jokes can be made out of the fact that Benedick has to change position to hear what is being said as the three move around the orchard?

2 The audience knows that Benedick can hear most of what is being said. Leonato, Claudio and Don Pedro try to make him feel interested in Beatrice.

a What can be made amusing about Benedick's reactions to some of the things his friends say about him?

b Which lines are written to be spoken quietly, so that Benedick doesn't hear them and realise that he is being tricked?

c Which lines do you think would be said especially loudly so that he is sure to hear them?

d Which lines show that the three friends enjoy the chance to wind up the listening Benedick, knowing that he can't reply without giving himself away?

3 How should the actor playing Don Pedro speak, move and behave at these points?

"See you where Benedick hath hid himself?"

"the man, as you know all, hath a contemptible spirit"

"He doth indeed show some sparks that are like wit."

4 How should the actor playing Claudio speak, move and behave at this point?

"O, ay: stalk on, stalk on; the fowl sits. I did never think that lady would have loved any man."

5 What directions would you give to the actor playing Benedick at these points?

> "I thank you for your pains"
>
> "Ha! 'Against my will I am sent to bid you come in to dinner'"

Practical work

Solo or in pairs

1 Read aloud Benedick's final speech in three different ways:

- to bring out a confident change of mind from the start
- to be unsure and doubtful throughout
- to be uncertain and then more sure.

Which words need different emphasis for each reading?

2 Try saying "The world must be peopled" as if:

- it is an unpleasant duty
- it is a sudden, happy discovery
- it is a very sensible, practical reason for not being selfish and staying a bachelor.

In groups

1 **Hot seat**

a Put Benedick in the hot seat and ask him why he has changed his view of Beatrice.

b Put Don Pedro in the hot seat and question him about his plan – and why he thought it would work.

2 **Tableau talkback**

The group freezes in a tableau of the scene in the garden. The questioner walks around the figures in the tableau and asks what different characters think about the situation.

3 Improvise a scene in which three of your friends want to get another friend to go out with a girl. The fourth friend says he doesn't like her. The three friends set up a situation where the fourth friend overhears them talking. What they say about him, and about the girl, must make him change his mind.

They could try to make him:

- prove something
- feel ashamed of himself
- feel that he's lucky to be fancied.

Try these two ways:

- the fourth friend is already on stage, facing the audience and the three others come on and pretend not to see him
- the three friends are on stage and the fourth one comes on.

Social, cultural and historical aspects

1 Is Benedick's attitude to marriage and staying single an attitude of Shakespeare's day or is it an attitude that exists today?

2 Is the change from liking "the drum and the fife" to preferring "the tabour and the pipe" an attitude of Shakespeare's day or is it familiar in some ways today?

Proving a point – from *The Taming of the Shrew*

Introduction

Katharina is the daughter of a rich merchant called Baptista. Her sister Bianca is obedient and charming, and Baptista thinks she would make an ideal wife for a suitable young man. Katharina is outspoken, independent and intelligent. She does not see why she should pretend to be pleased by men who are less intelligent than she is. Consequently, the men she meets find her proud and bad tempered – or "curst" as the expression was in Shakespeare's day.

Her father resolves to give money to any man who will marry her and tame her. Petruchio decides that he is the man for the task. He has studied books on training hawks and horses and dogs, and he thinks he is at least as clever as she is.

The following scenes show how his plan works. Petruchio humiliates Katharina in public at the wedding. He allows her no decent food or peace or comfort at home. He takes every chance to prove that he is the master.

The play ends with a bet between Petruchio and his friends about whose wife is the most obedient. Katharina turns out to be the only wife who obeys her husband, and she lectures the other wives about being respectful and obedient to their husbands.

The witty argument and some of the comic stage business make this an entertaining play in the theatre. But it does have a message about men and women that modern readers may strongly disagree with. Some actors and directors think the play is too offensive to be put on the stage today. Others have tried to present the play in a more sympathetic way to Katharina and to women in general.

Studying this text makes a modern reader think hard about the play as comic entertainment, and about values and attitudes that do not fit our own society and culture.

Henry Woodward as Petruchio in 'The Taming of the Shrew', 1775.

Script

Act II, Scene 1

Baptista's house

PETRUCHIO: I will attend her here,
And woo her with some spirit when she comes.
Say that she rail; why then I'll tell her plain
She sings as sweetly as a nightingale:
Say that she frown, I'll say she looks as clear
As morning roses newly wash'd with dew:
Say she be mute and will not speak a word;
Then I'll commend her volubility,
And say she uttereth piercing eloquence:
If she do bid me pack, I'll give her thanks,
As though she bid me stay by her a week:
If she deny to wed, I'll crave the day
When I shall ask the banns and when be married.
But here she comes; and now, Petruchio, speak.

Enter Katharina

Good morrow, Kate; for that's your name, I hear.

KATHARINA: Well have you heard, but something hard of hearing:
They call me Katharina that do talk of me.

PETRUCHIO: You lie, in faith; for you are call'd plain Kate,
And bonny Kate and sometimes Kate the curst;
But Kate, the prettiest Kate in Christendom,
Hearing thy mildness praised in every town,
Thy virtues spoke of, and thy beauty sounded,
Yet not so deeply as to thee belongs,
Myself am moved to woo thee for my wife.

KATHARINA: Moved! in good time: let him that moved you hither
Remove you hence: I knew you at the first
You were a moveable.

PETRUCHIO: Why, what's a moveable?

KATHARINA: A joint-stool.

PETRUCHIO: Thou hast hit it: come, sit on me.

KATHARINA: Asses are made to bear, and so are you.

PETRUCHIO: Women are made to bear, and so are you.

KATHARINA: No such a jade as you, if me you mean.

PETRUCHIO: Come, come, you wasp; i' faith, you are too angry.

KATHARINA: If I be waspish, best beware my sting.

PETRUCHIO: My remedy is then, to pluck it out.

KATHARINA: Ay, if the fool could find it where it lies.

PETRUCHIO: Who knows not where a wasp does wear his sting?
              In his tail.

KATHARINA: In his tongue.

PETRUCHIO: Whose tongue?

KATHARINA: Yours, if you talk of tales: and so farewell.

She turns to go

PETRUCHIO: What, with my tongue in your tail? nay, come again,

He seizes her in his arms

              Good Kate; I am a gentleman.

KATHARINA: That I'll try.

She strikes him

PETRUCHIO: I swear I'll cuff you, if you strike again.

KATHARINA: If you strike me, you are no gentleman.

PETRUCHIO: Nay, come, Kate, come; you must not look so sour.

KATHARINA: It is my fashion, when I see a crab.

PETRUCHIO: Why, here's no crab; and therefore look not sour.

KATHARINA: There is, there is.

PETRUCHIO: Then show it me.

KATHARINA: Had I a glass, I would.

PETRUCHIO: What, you mean my face?

KATHARINA: Well aim'd of such a young one.

She struggles

PETRUCHIO: Now, by Saint George, I am too young for you.

KATHARINA: Yet you are wither'd.

Petruchio touches his forehead

PETRUCHIO: 'Tis with cares.

Kisses her hand

KATHARINA: I care not.

She slips from him

PETRUCHIO: Nay, hear you, Kate: in sooth you scape not so.

He catches her once more

KATHARINA: I chafe you, if I tarry: let me go.

She struggles again, biting and scratching as he speaks

PETRUCHIO: No, not a whit: I find you passing gentle.
              'Twas told me you were rough and coy and sullen,

And now I find report a very liar;
For thou art pleasant, gamesome, passing courteous,
But slow in speech, yet sweet as spring-time flowers:
Thou canst not frown, thou canst not look askance,
Nor bite the lip, as angry wenches will,
Nor hast thou pleasure to be cross in talk,
But thou with mildness entertain'st thy wooers,
With gentle conference, soft and affable.

He releases her

KATHARINA: Go, fool, and whom thou keep'st command.
Where did you study all this goodly speech?

PETRUCHIO: It is extempore, from my mother-wit.

KATHARINA: A witty mother! witless else her son.

PETRUCHIO: Am I not wise?

KATHARINA: Yes; keep you warm.

PETRUCHIO: Marry, so I mean, sweet Katharine, in thy bed:
And therefore, setting all this chat aside,
Thus in plain terms: your father hath consented
That you shall be my wife; your dowry 'greed on;
And, will you, nill you, I will marry you.
Now, Kate, I am a husband for your turn;
For, by this light, whereby I see thy beauty,
Thy beauty, that doth make me like thee well,
Thou must be married to no man but me;
For I am he am born to tame you Kate,
And bring you from a wild Kate to a Kate
Conformable as other household Kates.
Here comes your father: never make denial;
I must and will have Katharine to my wife.

Enter Baptista

BAPTISTA: Now, Signior Petruchio, how speed you with my
daughter?

PETRUCHIO: How but well, sir? how but well?
It were impossible I should speed amiss.

BAPTISTA: Why, how now, daughter Katharine! in your dumps?

KATHARINA: Call you me daughter? now, I promise you
You have show'd a tender fatherly regard,
To wish me wed to one half lunatic;
A mad-cap ruffian and a swearing Jack,
That thinks with oaths to face the matter out.

PETRUCHIO: Father, 'tis thus: yourself and all the world,
That talk'd of her, have talk'd amiss of her:
For she's not froward, but modest as the dove;

	And to conclude, we have 'greed so well together,
	That upon Sunday is the wedding-day.
KATHARINA:	I'll see thee hang'd on Sunday first.
BAPTISTA:	Hark, Petruchio; she says she'll see thee hang'd first.
PETRUCHIO:	I tell you, 'tis incredible to believe
	How much she loves me: O, the kindest Kate!
	She hung about my neck; and kiss on kiss
	She vied so fast, protesting oath on oath,
	That in a twink she won me to her love.
	Provide the feast, father, and bid the guests;
	Give me thy hand, Kate: I will unto Venice,

He snatches her hand

	To buy apparel 'gainst the wedding-day.
	We will have rings and things and fine array;
	And kiss me, Kate, we will be married o' Sunday.
BAPTISTA:	I know not what to say: but give me your hands;
	God send you joy, Petruchio! 'tis a match.

Exeunt Petruchio and Katharina severally

*The wedding is arranged. Katharina and her father
reach the altar on Sunday but Petruchio doesn't turn up.
Katharina and her father go back home, to find Petruchio
dressed scruffily. He insists on going back to the church
without changing, "an eyesore" to the ceremony. They go
back to the church where Petruchio insults the priest
and spills wine over the sexton. Instead of a wedding
reception, he takes her straight back to his home.*

Act IV, Scene 1

At Petruchio's house

Enter Petruchio and Katharina

PETRUCHIO:	Where be these knaves? What, no man at door
	To hold my stirrup nor to take my horse!
	Where is Nathaniel, Gregory, Philip?
ALL SERVING-MEN:	Here, here, sir; here, sir.
PETRUCHIO:	Here, sir! here, sir! here, sir! here, sir!
	You logger-headed and unpolish'd grooms!
	What, no attendance? no regard? no duty?
	Where is the foolish knave I sent before?
GRUMIO:	Here, sir; as foolish as I was before.
PETRUCHIO:	You peasant swain! you whoreson malt-horse drudge!
	Did I not bid thee meet me in the park,

And bring along these rascal knaves with thee?
Go, rascals, go, and fetch my supper in.

Exeunt Servants

(Singing)
'Where is the life that late I led—'
Where are those *(seeing Katharina still at the door)* – Sit
down, Kate, and welcome. –

He brings her to the fire

Food, food, food, food!

Re-enter Servants with supper

Why, when, I say? Nay, good sweet Kate, be merry.

He sits beside her

Off with my boots, you rogues! you villains, when?

A servant kneels to take off his boots

(Sings)
'It was the friar of orders grey,
As he forth walked on his way:—'
Out, you rogue! you pluck my foot awry:

Strike him

Take that, and mend the plucking off the other.

The second boot is removed. He rises

Be merry, Kate. Some water, here; what, ho!

Enter a servant with water. Petruchio looks away

Where's my spaniel Troilus? Sirrah, get you hence,
And bid my cousin Ferdinand come hither:
One, Kate, that you must kiss, and be acquainted with.
Where are my slippers? Shall I have some water?

The basin is presented a second time

Come, Kate, and wash, and welcome heartily.

(He stumbles against the servant and spills the water)
You whoreson villain! will you let it fall?

(He strikes him)

KATHARINA: Patience, I pray you; 'twas a fault unwilling.

PETRUCHIO: A whoreson beetle-headed, flap-ear'd knave!
Come, Kate, sit down; I know you have a stomach.

She comes to the table

Will you give thanks, sweet Kate; or else shall I?
What's this? mutton?

FIRST SERVANT: Ay.

PETRUCHIO: Who brought it?

PETER: I.

PETRUCHIO: 'Tis burnt; and so is all the meat.
What dogs are these! Where is the rascal cook?
How durst you, villains, bring it from the dresser,
And serve it thus to me that love it not?
There take it to you, trenchers, cups, and all;

He throws the meal at the Servants' heads

You heedless joltheads and unmanner'd slaves!
What, do you grumble? I'll be with you straight.

Exeunt Servants

KATHARINA: I pray you, husband, be not so disquiet:
The meat was well, if you were so contented.

PETRUCHIO: I tell thee, Kate, 'twas burnt and dried away;
And I expressly am forbid to touch it,
For it engenders choler, planteth anger;
And better 'twere that both of us did fast,
Since, of ourselves, ourselves are choleric,
Than feed it with such over-roasted flesh.
Be patient; to-morrow 't shall be mended,
And, for this night, we'll fast for company:
Come, I will bring thee to thy bridal chamber.

Exeunt
Re-enter Servants severally

NATHANIEL: Peter, didst ever see the like?

GRUMIO: Where is he?

CURTIS: In her chamber, making a sermon of continency to her;
And rails, and swears, and rates, that she, poor soul,
Knows not which way to stand, to look, to speak,
And sits as one new-risen from a dream.
Away, away! for he is coming hither.

Exeunt
Re-enter Petruchio

PETRUCHIO: Thus have I politicly begun my reign,
And 'tis my hope to end successfully.
My falcon now is sharp and passing empty;
And till she stoop she must not be full-gorged,
For then she never looks upon her lure.
Another way I have to man my haggard,
To make her come and know her keeper's call,
That is, to watch her, as we watch these kites
That bate and beat and will not be obedient.
She eat no meat to-day, nor none shall eat;
Last night she slept not, nor to-night she shall not;
As with the meat, some undeserved fault

Josie Lawrence in 'The Taming of the Shrew' in modern dress.

I'll find about the making of the bed;
And here I'll fling the pillow, there the bolster,
This way the coverlet, another way the sheets:
Ay, and amid this hurly I intend
That all is done in reverend care of her;
And in conclusion she shall watch all night:
And if she chance to nod I'll rail and brawl
And with the clamour keep her still awake.
This is a way to kill a wife with kindness;
And thus I'll curb her mad and headstrong humour.
He that knows better how to tame a shrew,
Now let him speak: 'tis charity to show.

Exit

Act V, Scene 2

At Baptista's after supper, with guests

BAPTISTA: Now, in good sadness, son Petrucio,
I think thou has the veriest shrew of all.

PETRUCHIO: Well, I say no: and therefore for assurance
Let's each one send unto his wife;
And he whose wife is most obedient
To come at first when he doth send for her,
Shall win the wager which we will propose.

HORTENSIO: Content. What is the wager?

LUCENTIO: Twenty crowns.

PETRUCHIO: Twenty crowns!
I'll venture so much of my hawk or hound,
But twenty times so much upon my wife.

LUCENTIO: A hundred then.

HORTENSIO: Content.

PETRUCHIO: A match! 'tis done.

HORTENSIO: Who shall begin?

LUCENTIO: That will I.
Go, servant, bid your mistress come to me.

SERVANT: I go.

Exit

BAPTISTA: Son, I'll be your half, Bianca comes.

LUCENTIO: I'll have no halves; I'll bear it all myself.

Re-enter Servant

How now! what news?

SERVANT:	Sir, my mistress sends you word That she is busy and she cannot come.
PETRUCHIO:	How! she is busy and she cannot come! Is that an answer?
GRUMIO:	Ay, and a kind one too: Pray God, sir, your wife send you not a worse.
PETRUCHIO:	I hope better.
HORTENSIO:	Sirrah, go and entreat my wife To come to me forthwith.

Exit Servant

PETRUCHIO:	O, ho! entreat her! Nay, then she must needs come.
HORTENSIO:	I am afraid, sir, Do what you can, yours will not be entreated.

Re-enter Servant

	Now, where's my wife?
SERVANT:	She says you have some goodly jest in hand: She will not come: she bids you come to her.
PETRUCHIO:	Worse and worse; she will not come! O vile, Intolerable, not to be endured! Sirrah Grumio, go to your mistress; Say, I command her to come to me.

Exit Grumio

HORTENSIO:	I know her answer.
PETRUCHIO:	What?
HORTENSIO:	She will not.
PETRUCHIO:	The fouler fortune mine, and there an end.
BAPTISTA:	Now, by my holidame, here comes Katharina!

Re-enter Katharina

KATHARINA:	What is your will, sir, that you send for me?
PETRUCHIO:	Where is your sister, and Hortensio's wife?
KATHARINA:	They sit conferring by the parlour fire.
PETRUCHIO:	Go fetch then hither unto their husbands: Away, I say, and bring them hither straight.

Exit Katharina

LUCENTIO:	Here is a wonder, if you talk of a wonder.
HORTENSIO:	And so it is: I wonder what it bodes.
PETRUCHIO:	Marry, peace it bodes, and love and quiet life, And awful rule and right supremacy;

And, to be short, what not, that's sweet and happy?

BAPTISTA: Now, fair befal thee, good Petruchio!
The wager thou hast won; and I will add
Unto their losses twenty thousand crowns;
Another dowry to another daughter,
For she is changed, as she had never been.

PETRUCHIO: Nay, I will win my wager better yet
And show more sign of her obedience,
Her new-built virtue and obedience.
See where she comes and brings your froward wives
As prisoners to her womanly persuasion.

Re-enter Katharina, with Bianca and Hortensio's wife

Katharine, that cap of yours becomes you not:
Off with that bauble, throw it under-foot.

HORTENSIO'S WIFE: Lord, let me never have a cause to sigh,
Till I be brought to such a silly pass!

BIANCA: Fie! what a foolish duty call you this?

LUCENTIO: I would your duty were as foolish too:
The wisdom of your duty, fair Bianca,
Hath cost one hundred crowns since supper-time.

BIANCA: The more fool you, for laying on my duty.

PETRUCHIO: Katharine, I charge thee, tell these headstrong women
What duty they do owe their lords and husbands.

HORTENSIO'S WIFE: Come, come, you're mocking: we will have no telling.

PETRUCHIO: Come on, I say; and first begin with her.

HORTENSIO'S WIFE: She shall not.

PETRUCHIO: I say she shall: and first begin with her.

KATHARINA: Fie, fie! unknit that threatening unkind brow,
And dart not scornful glances from those eyes,
To wound thy lord, thy king, thy governor:
It blots thy beauty as frosts do bite the meads,
Confounds thy fame as whirlwinds shake fair buds,
And in no sense is meet or amiable.
A woman moved is like a fountain troubled,
Muddy, ill-seeming, thick, bereft of beauty;
And while it is so, none so dry or thirsty
Will deign to sip or touch one drop of it.
Thy husband is thy lord, thy life, thy keeper,
Thy head, thy sovereign; one that cares for thee,
And for thy maintenance commits his body
To painful labour both by sea and land,
To watch the night in storms, the day in cold,
Whilst thou liest warm at home, secure and safe;

And craves no other tribute at thy hands
But love, fair looks and true obedience;
Too little payment for so great a debt.
Such duty as the subject owes the prince
Even such a woman oweth to her husband;
And when she is froward, peevish, sullen, sour,
And not obedient to his honest will,
What is she but a foul contending rebel
And graceless traitor to her loving lord?
I am ashamed that women are so simple
To offer war where they should kneel for peace;
Or seek for rule, supremacy and sway,
When they are bound to serve, love and obey.
Why are our bodies soft and weak and smooth,
Unapt to toil and trouble in the world,
But that our soft conditions and our hearts
Should well agree with our external parts?
Come, come, you froward and unable worms!
My mind hath been as big as one of yours,
My heart as great, my reason haply more,
To bandy word for word and frown for frown;
But now I see our lances are but straws,
Our strength as weak, our weakness past compare,
That seeming to be most which we indeed least are.
Then vail your stomachs, for it is no boot,
And place your hands below your husband's foot:
In token of which duty, if he please,
My hand is ready; may it do him ease.

PETRUCHIO: Why, there's a wench! Come on, and kiss me, Kate.
Come, Kate, we'll to bed.
We three are married, but you two are sped.
'Twas I won the wager, though you hit the white;
And, being a winner, God give you good night!

Exeunt Petruchio and Katharina

HORTENSIO: Now, go thy ways; thou hast tamed a curst shrew.

LUCENTIO: 'Tis a wonder, by your leave, she will be tamed so.

Exeunt

Postscript

Purpose
- to entertain and amuse
- to explore relationships between men and women

Effects
- laughter at Petruchio's extreme behaviour
- sympathy with Katharina

Devices
- verbal wit
- comic action
- aside
- soliloquy

Glossary

rail	speak abusively
banns	public notice of wedding
curst	irritable and bad-tempered
moveable	piece of furniture (someone who is changeable)
jade	worn-out old horse
crab	a sour apple
tarry	wait, take time
affable	kind and polite
extempore	made up on the spot
froward	perverse and difficult
apparel	clothes
logger-headed	thick-headed
swain	lover
malt-horse	heavy horse used for pulling
trenchers	dinner-plates
engenders choler	leads to bad temper
continency	doing without
politicly	subtly, craftily
haggard	wild female hawk (from falconry)
bate	struggle to get away (from falconry)
holidame	mild religious oath – by my Holy Damne
meet	appropriate
peevish	irritable
vail	put down
stomachs	grievances (bellyaches)
boot	gain, advantage
hit the white	hit the centre of a target

Close-up on language

1 Make a list of terms of abuse that are unfamiliar today. (Some of them may be worth bringing back into use!)

2 Make a list of words that have double meanings.

Understanding character

Getting into thoughts and feelings

When Petruchio says "thou art pleasant, gamesome, passing courteous", he clearly does not believe what he is saying. On the other hand, when he says "Come on, and kiss me, Kate", perhaps he has genuine feelings for his wife.

1 What is Katharina thinking and feeling at these points?

> "Well have you heard, but something hard of hearing.
> They call me Katharina that do talk of me"
>
> "Moved!"
>
> "You were a moveable (...)
> A joint-stool"
>
> "and so farewell"
>
> "That I'll try."
>
> PETRUCHIO: "thou art pleasant, gamesome, passing courteous"
>
> "Call you me daughter?"
>
> PETRUCHIO: "I tell you 'tis incredible to believe
> How much she loves me"
>
> "Patience, I pray you; 'twas a fault unwilling"
>
> "The meat was well, if you were so contented"

2 What is Petruchio thinking and feeling at these points?

> "Good morrow, Kate; for that's your name, I hear"
>
> "Thy virtues spoke of (...)
> Yet not so deeply as to thee belongs"
>
> "Thou hast hit it: come, sit on me."
>
> "Women are made to bear, and so are you."
>
> "Why, here's no crab; and therefore look not sour."

3 What is Baptista thinking and feeling at this point?

> "Now, Signior Petruchio, how speed you with my daughter?"

Social, cultural and historical aspects

1 What would make these scenes entertaining to an Elizabethan audience? Think of character, action, situation, language and ideas.

2 Would they be as entertaining to a modern audience?

How would you treat this script to make it seem relevant and acceptable to a modern audience?

Think of:

- editing the text
- casting the play
- directing the performance
- advertising it in the press and on TV.

Alternating sympathies – from
The Merchant of Venice

'The Merchant of Venice', 1989, showing Geraldine James, Leigh Lawson and Dustin Hoffman.

Introduction

Shylock is a Jewish resident of Venice, a city that doesn't allow non-Venetians to take up many trades and professions. Like other Jews facing this problem, he makes a living by money-lending.

Shylock feels isolated and rejected by the Venetian community, and his loneliness is made worse by the death of his wife, Leah. He brings up Jessica, his only child, strictly, trying to protect her from the outside world and trying to keep her in the Jewish tradition. Like many daughters, she rebels against this, and she falls in love with Lorenzo, a Christian.

The audience's sympathies are divided between understanding Shylock's isolation and resentment, and understanding Jessica's need for social life, and her rebelliousness.

In these scenes, the audience's attitude shifts according to Shylock's attitudes and the attitudes of those around him. He is not perfect by any means, but he is not a bad man. Others are not bad men, but they are not perfect either. Shakespeare shows us that feelings, motives and relationships are more complicated than they first appear. He lets us see both sides of the parent–daughter relationship, and both sides of the outsider–insider relationship in a community. As well as this, he shows us the effects of racism and economics.

In such a place, such sum or sums as are
Express'd in the condition, let the forfeit
Be nominated for an equal pound
Of your fair flesh, to be cut off and taken
In what part of your body pleaseth me.

ANTONIO: Content, i' faith: I'll seal to such a bond
And say there is much kindness in the Jew.

BASSANIO: You shall not seal to such a bond for me:
I'll rather dwell in my necessity.

ANTONIO: Why, fear not, man; I will not forfeit it:
Within these two months, that's a month before
This bond expires, I do expect return
Of thrice three times the value of this bond.

SHYLOCK: O father Abram, what these Christians are,
Whose own hard dealings teaches them suspect
The thoughts of others! Pray you, tell me this;
If he should break his day, what should I gain
By the exaction of the forfeiture?
A pound of man's flesh taken from a man
Is not so estimable, profitable neither,
As flesh of muttons, beefs, or goats. I say,
To buy his favour, I extend this friendship:
If he will take it, so; if not, adieu;
And, for my love, I pray you wrong me not.

ANTONIO: Yes Shylock, I will seal unto this bond.

SHYLOCK: Then meet me forthwith at the notary's;
Give him direction for this merry bond,
And I will go and purse the ducats straight,
See to my house, left in the fearful guard
Of an unthrifty knave, and presently
I will be with you.

ANTONIO: Hie thee, gentle Jew.

Exit Shylock

The Hebrew will turn Christian: he grows kind.

BASSANIO: I like not fair terms and a villain's mind.

ANTONIO: Come on: in this there can be no dismay;
My ships come home a month before the day.

Exeunt

Act II, Scene 5

Before Shylock's house

Enter Shylock and Launcelot

SHYLOCK:	Well, thou shalt see, thy eyes shall be thy judge,
	The difference of old Shylock and Bassanio: –
	What, Jessica! – thou shalt not gormandise,
	As thou hast done with me: – What, Jessica! –
	And sleep and snore, and rend apparel out; –
	Why, Jessica, I say!

Enter Jessica

JESSICA:	Call you? what is your will?
SHYLOCK:	I am bid forth to supper, Jessica:
	There are my keys. But wherefore should I go?
	I am not bid for love; they flatter me:
	But yet I'll go in hate, to feed upon
	The prodigal Christian. Jessica, my girl,
	Look to my house. I am right loath to go:
	There is some ill a-brewing towards my rest,
	For I did dream of money-bags to-night.
LAUNCELOT:	I beseech you, sir, go: my young master doth
	expect your reproach.
SHYLOCK:	So do I his.
LAUNCELOT:	An they have conspired together, I will not say you
	shall see a masque; but if you do, then it was not
	for nothing that my nose fell a-bleeding on
	Black-Monday last at six o'clock i' the morning,
	falling out that year on Ash-Wednesday was four
	year, in the afternoon.
SHYLOCK:	What, are there masques? Hear you me, Jessica:
	Lock up my doors; and when you hear the drum
	And the vile squealing of the wry-neck'd fife,
	Clamber not you up to the casements then,
	Nor thrust your head into the public street
	To gaze on Christian fools with varnish'd faces,
	But stop my house's ears, I mean my casements:
	Let not the sound of shallow foppery enter
	My sober house. By Jacob's staff, I swear,
	I have no mind of feasting forth to-night:
	But I will go. Go you before me, sirrah;
	Say I will come.
LAUNCELOT:	I will go before, sir.
	Mistress, look out at window, for all this,
	There will come a Christian by,
	Will be worth a Jewess' eye.

Exit

SHYLOCK:	What says that fool of Hagar's offspring, ha?
JESSICA:	His words were 'Farewell mistress'; nothing else.
SHYLOCK:	The patch is kind enough, but a huge feeder;
	Snail-slow in profit, and he sleeps by day
	More than the wild-cat: drones hive not with me;
	Therefore I part with him, and part with him
	To one that I would have him help to waste
	His borrow'd purse. Well, Jessica, go in;
	Perhaps I will return immediately:
	Do as I bid you; shut doors after you:
	Fast bind, fast find;
	A proverb never stale in thrifty mind.

Exit

JESSICA:	Farewell; and if my fortune be not crost,
	I have a father, you a daughter, lost.

Exit

Act III, Scene 1

SHYLOCK:	How now, Tubal! what news from Genoa? hast thou found my daughter?
TUBAL:	I often came where I did hear of her, but cannot find her.
SHYLOCK:	Why, there, there, there, there! a diamond gone, cost me two thousand ducats in Frankfort! The curse never fell upon our nation till now; I never felt it till now: two thousands ducats in that; and other precious, precious jewels. I would my daughter were dead at my foot, and the jewels in her ear! would she were hearsed at my foot, and the ducats in her coffin! No news of them? Why, so: and I know not what's spent in the search: why, thou loss upon loss! the thief gone with so much, and so much to find the thief; and no satisfaction, no revenge: nor no ill luck stirring but what lights on my shoulders; no sighs but of my breathing; no tears but of my shedding.
TUBAL:	Yes, other men have ill luck too: Antonio, as I heard in Genoa,—
SHYLOCK:	What, what, what? ill luck, ill luck?
TUBAL:	Hath an argosy cast away, coming from Tripolis.
SHYLOCK:	I thank God, I thank God. Is't true, is't true?
TUBAL:	I spoke with some of the sailors that escaped the wreck.

SHYLOCK: I thank thee, good Tubal: good news, good news! ha, ha! where? in Genoa?

TUBAL: Your daughter spent in Genoa, as I heard, in one night fourscore ducats.

SHYLOCK: Thou stickest a dagger in me: I shall never see my gold again: fourscore ducats at a sitting! fourscore ducats!

TUBAL: There came divers of Antonio's creditors in my company to Venice, that swear he cannot choose but break.

SHYLOCK: I am very glad of it: I'll plague him; I'll torture him: I am glad of it.

TUBAL: One of them showed me a ring that he had of your daughter for a monkey.

SHYLOCK: Out upon her! Thou torturest me, Tubal: it was my turquoise; I had it of Leah when I was a bachelor: I would not have given it for a wilderness of monkeys.

TUBAL: But Antonio is certainly undone.

SHYLOCK: Nay, that's true, that's very true. Go, Tubal, fee me an officer; bespeak him a fortnight before. I will have the heart of him, if he forfeit; for, were he out of Venice, I can make what merchandise I will. Go, go, Tubal, and meet me at our synagogue; go, good Tubal; at our synagogue, Tubal.

Exeunt

Act IV, Scene 1

ANTONIO: Most heartily I do beseech the court
To give the judgment.

PORTIA: Why then, thus it is:
You must prepare your bosom for his knife.

SHYLOCK: O noble judge! O excellent young man!

PORTIA: For the intent and purpose of the law
Hath full relation to the penalty,
Which here appeareth due upon the bond.

SHYLOCK: 'Tis very true: O wise and upright judge!
How much more elder art thou than thy looks!

PORTIA: Therefore lay bare your bosom.

SHYLOCK: Ay, his breast:
So says the bond: doth it not, noble judge?
'Nearest his heart': those are the very words.

PORTIA: It is so. Are there balance here to weigh
The flesh?

SHYLOCK: I have them ready.

PORTIA: Have by some surgeon, Shylock, on your charge,
             To stop his wounds, lest he do bleed to death.

SHYLOCK: Is it so nominated in the bond?

PORTIA: It is not so express'd: but what of that?
             'Twere good you do so much for charity.

SHYLOCK: I cannot find it; 'tis not in the bond.

PORTIA: You, merchant, have you any thing to say?

ANTONIO: But little: I am arm'd and well prepared.
             Give me your hand, Bassanio: fare you well!
             Grieve not that I am fallen to this for you;
             For herein Fortune shows herself more kind
             Than is her custom: it is still her use
             To let the wretched man outlive his wealth,
             To view with hollow eye and wrinkled brow
             An age of poverty; from which lingering penance
             Of such misery doth she cut me off.
             Commend me to your honourable wife:
             Tell her the process of Antonio's end;
             Say how I loved you, speak me fair in death;
             And, when the tale is told, bid her be judge
             Whether Bassanio had not once a love.
             Repent but you that you shall lose your friend,
             And he repents not that he pays your debt;
             For if the Jew do cut but deep enough,
             I'll pay it presently with all my heart.

BASSANIO: Antonio, I am married to a wife
             Which is as dear to me as life itself;
             But life itself, my wife, and all the world,
             Are not with me esteem'd above thy life:
             I would lose all, ay, sacrifice them all
             Here to this devil, to deliver you.

PORTIA: Your wife would give you little thanks for that,
             If she were by, to hear you make the offer.

GRATIANO: I have a wife, whom, I protest, I love:
             I would she were in heaven, so she could
             Entreat some power to change this currish Jew.

NERISSA: 'Tis well you offer it behind her back;
             The wish would make else an unquiet house.

SHYLOCK: *Aside* These be the Christian husbands. I have a daughter;
             Would any of the stock of Barrabas
             Had been her husband rather than a Christian!

             Aloud We trifle time: I pray thee, pursue sentence.

Dame Ellen Terry as Portia in 'The Merchant of Venice'.

PORTIA: A pound of that same merchant's flesh is thine:
            The court awards it, and the law doth give it.

SHYLOCK: Most rightful judge!

PORTIA: And you must cut this flesh from off his breast:
            The law allows it, and the court awards it.

SHYLOCK: Most learned judge! A sentence! Come, prepare!

PORTIA: Tarry a little; there is something else.
            This bond doth give thee here no jot of blood;
            The words expressly are 'a pound of flesh':
            Take then thy bond, take thou thy pound of flesh;
            But, in the cutting it, if thou dost shed
            One drop of Christian blood, thy lands and goods
            Are, by the laws of Venice, confiscate
            Unto the state of Venice.

GRATIANO: O upright judge! Mark, Jew: O learned judge!

SHYLOCK: Is that the law?

PORTIA: Thyself shalt see the act:
            For, as thou urgest justice, be assured
            Thou shalt have justice, more than thou desirest.

GRATIANO: O learned judge! Mark, Jew: a learned judge!

SHYLOCK: I take this offer, then; pay the bond thrice
            And let the Christian go.

BASSANIO: Here is the money.

PORTIA: Soft!
            The Jew shall have all justice; soft! no haste:
            He shall have nothing but the penalty.

GRATIANO: O Jew! an upright judge, a learned judge!

PORTIA: Therefore prepare thee to cut off the flesh.
            Shed thou no blood, nor cut thou less nor more
            But just a pound of flesh: if thou tak'st more
            Or less than a just pound, be it but so much
            As makes it light or heavy in the substance,
            Or the division of the twentieth part
            Of one poor scruple, nay, if the scale do turn
            But in the estimation of a hair,
            Thou diest and all thy goods are confiscate.

GRATIANO: A second Daniel, a Daniel, Jew!
            Now, infidel, I have you on the hip.

PORTIA: Why doth the Jew pause? take thy forfeiture.

SHYLOCK: Give me my principal, and let me go.

BASSANIO: I have it ready for thee; here it is.

PORTIA:	He hath refused it in the open court:
	He shall have merely justice and his bond.
GRATIANO:	A Daniel, still say I, a second Daniel!
	I thank thee, Jew, for teaching me that word.
SHYLOCK:	Shall I not have barely my principal?
PORTIA:	Thou shalt have nothing but the forfeiture,
	To be so taken at thy peril, Jew.
SHYLOCK:	Why, then the devil give him good of it!
	I'll stay no longer question.
PORTIA:	Tarry, Jew:
	The law hath yet another hold on you.
	It is enacted in the laws of Venice,
	If it be proved against an alien
	That by direct or indirect attempts
	He seek the life of any citizen,
	The party 'gainst the which he doth contrive
	Shall seize one half his goods; the other half
	Comes to the privy coffer of the state;
	And the offender's life lies in the mercy
	Of the duke only, 'gainst all other voice.
	In which predicament, I say, thou stand'st;
	For it appears, by manifest proceeding,
	That indirectly and directly too
	Thou hast contrived against the very life
	Of the defendant; and thou hast incurr'd
	The danger formerly by me rehearsed.
	Down therefore and beg mercy of the duke.
GRATIANO:	Beg that thou mayst have leave to hang thyself:
	And yet, thy wealth being forfeit to the state,
	Thou hast not left the value of a cord;
	Therefore thou must be hang'd at the state's charge.
DUKE:	That thou shalt see the difference of our spirits,
	I pardon thee thy life before thou ask it:
	For half thy wealth, it is Antonio's;
	The other half comes to the general state,
	Which humbleness may drive unto a fine.
PORTIA:	Ay, for the state, not for Antonio.
SHYLOCK:	Nay, take my life and all; pardon not that:
	You take my house when you do take the prop
	That doth sustain my house; you take my life
	When you do take the means whereby I live.
PORTIA:	What mercy can you render him, Antonio?
GRATIANO:	A halter gratis; nothing else, for God's sake.

ANTONIO:	So please my lord the duke and all the court
	To quit the fine for one half of his goods,
	I am content; so he will let me have
	The other half in use, to render it,
	Upon his death, unto the gentleman
	That lately stole his daughter:
	Two things provided more, that, for this favour,
	He presently become a Christian;
	The other, that he do record a gift,
	Here in the court, of all he dies possess'd,
	Unto his son Lorenzo and his daughter.
DUKE:	He shall do this, or else I do recant
	The pardon that I late pronounced here.
PORTIA:	Art thou contented, Jew? what dost thou say?
SHYLOCK:	I am content.
PORTIA:	Clerk, draw a deed of gift.
SHYLOCK:	I pray you, give me leave to go from hence;
	I am not well: send the deed after me,
	And I will sign it.
DUKE:	Get thee gone, but do it.
GRATIANO:	In christening shalt thou have two god-fathers:
	Had I been judge, thou shouldst have had ten more,
	To bring thee to the gallows, not the font.

Exit Shylock

Postscript

Purpose
- to create dramatic conflict and suspense
- to explore motives and the difference between justice and mercy

Effects
- sympathy with Shylock as an abused outsider
- sympathy with Jessica as victim of a strict father
- sympathy with Antonio as a victim of bad luck

Devices
- contrasting scenes/contrasting emotions
- character in disguise
- dramatic irony
- aside

Glossary

ducat	Venetian money
exhibit	show
get	beget (cause you to be born)
heinous	vile and hateful
usance	interest charged on loans
sufferance	enduring pain and misfortune
gaberdine	loose woollen frock-coat worn by Jews in Shakespeare's day
void your rheum	spit
spurn	reject with contempt
cur	a mongrel dog
bondman	servant
doit	a tiny amount
kind	in kind, in goods rather than money
notary	legal official
gormandise	eat greedily
rend	tear
apparel	clothing
prodigal	reckless with money
loath	unwilling
masque	dramatic entertainment
wry-neck'd fife	musical instrument
casements	windows
foppery	foolish behaviour
Hagar's offspring	illegitimate son (of Abraham's concubine)
patch	fool
drones	male bees (not workers)
argosy	merchant ship
fourscore	eighty
divers	various
turquoise	bluish precious stone
tarry	wait, take your time
scruple	a tiny amount
infidel	unbeliever
principal	original sum of money loaned
halter	a rope with a noose
gratis	free
recant	withdraw a previous statement

Close-up on language

1 Which words does Shylock use when talking to Antonio to make him feel ashamed?

2 Which words show Shylock's attitude that entertainment and pleasure are sinful or dangerous?

3 Which words reveal Shylock's contempt for people who don't look after their money?

Understanding character

Getting into thoughts and feelings

When Shylock says "Thou stickest a dagger in me: I shall never see my gold again", what he says is what he feels. He expresses his pain and real feelings. On the other hand, when he says "I would be friends with you and have your love" he may be concealing his true feelings. The actor and director must decide if he is already plotting revenge or not.

1 What is in Jessica's mind at these points?

> "I am sorry thou wilt leave my father so:
> Our house is hell, and thou, a merry devil"
>
> "I would not have my father
> See me in talk with thee"
>
> "though I am a daughter to his blood,
> I am not to his manners"
>
> SHYLOCK: "Clamber not you up to the casements then..."

2 What is in Shylock's mind at these points?

> "Still have I borne it with a patient shrug,
> For sufferance is the badge of all our tribe."
>
> "moneys is your suit
> What should I say to you?"
>
> "I would be friends with you and have your love"
>
> "What, what, what? ill luck, ill luck?"

3 What is Antonio thinking and feeling at these points?

> "lend it rather to thine enemy"
>
> "Why, fear not, man; I will not forfeit it"
>
> "The Hebrew will turn Christian: he grows kind"

4 What is Bassanio thinking and feeling at these points?

> "You shall not seal to such a bond for me"
>
> "I like not fair terms and a villain's mind."

Understanding performance

Staging and directing

1 What should the actor playing Jessica do at these points?

> "I would not have my father
> See me in talk with thee"

> "His words were 'Farewell, mistress'; nothing else."

2 What should the actor playing Shylock do at these points?

> "Why, there, there, there, there!"

> "I cannot find it; 'tis not in the bond."

Practical work

Solo or in pairs

1 Read the lines "What should I say to you (…) much moneys":
- with angry hatred
- with hurt and complaint
- with calm reasoned explanation.

Which is best?

2 Read the lines "Why, look you, how you storm (…) This is kind I offer", exaggerating the tone of:
- honest effort to win friends
- cunning effort to trap him by false friendship.

Which is better?

3 Design a theatre poster or video cover showing Shylock standing in the court surrounded by the others. What details of clothing and appearance would you use to bring out the difference between him and the other characters?

In groups

1 **Hot seat**

a Put Jessica in the hot seat and question her about her reasons for running away from home.

b Put Antonio in the hot seat and question him about his attitude to Shylock.

c Put Shylock in the hot seat and question him about his reasons for choosing the unusual bond. Ask him how he feels about Portia's courtroom plan and how he feels about the court's verdict.

2 **Tableau talkback**

The group freezes in a tableau of the scene in the courtroom. The questioner walks around the figures in the tableau and asks what different characters think about the situation.

3 Perform the section where Shylock forbids Jessica to watch the masque. Jessica has no lines: how may she react to her father's stern instruction?

4 Perform the section where Bassanio and Gratiano proclaim a love for Antonio greater than for their wives, unaware that Portia and Nerissa are present, disguised as lawyers.

Social, cultural and historical aspects

1 What do these scenes tell an audience about daily life in Venice, as Shakespeare presents it?

2 What do these scenes tell an audience about ideas and attitudes in Shakespeare's day?

3 What events in our society and in our time could be seen as similar to or different from those in these scenes?

Three early nineteenth century portraits of the actor Edmund Kean as Richard III.

Weighing up the choices – from *Measure for Measure*

Introduction

Lord Angelo is the Deputy to the Duke of Vienna. He has been put in charge of the city in the Duke's absence and he is determined to show that he can be a strong ruler. He was chosen to be Deputy because of his reputation for self-discipline, fasting and study. He thinks the people of Vienna have been ignoring the city's laws. One law that he decides to enforce is the law against sexual relationships outside marriage. When Claudio is caught in a sexual relationship, Angelo sees his chance to make an example of someone. He condemns Claudio to death.

Isabella is Claudio's brother. She is a young woman who believes in truth and purity, and wants to become a nun. She believes that sex outside marriage is a sin, and that people will be punished for committing this sin by losing their souls and going to hell. She disapproves of her brother's behaviour but she does not want him to be executed for it.

Angelo is surprised to find that Isabella has such an effect on him. He finds her sexually attractive, partly because she is so innocent and virtuous. Although he has condemned others for not controlling their sexual passion, he now cannot stop thinking of his sexual passion for her. He offers to save Claudio's life in exchange for

'Measure for Measure' performed by the Royal Shakespeare Company in 1991.

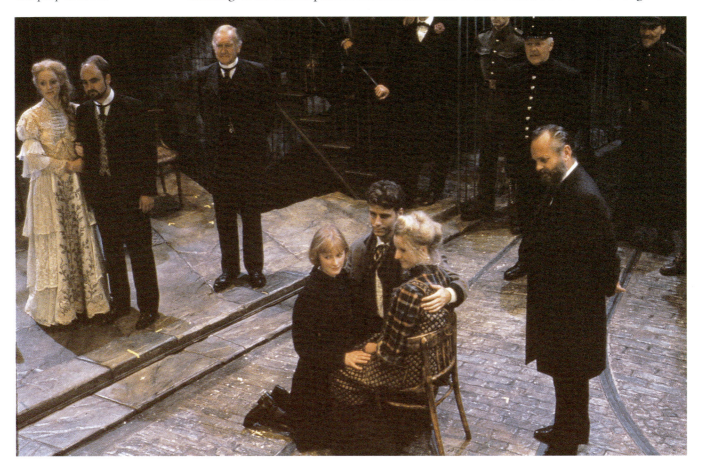

sex with Isabella. When she realises that this is what he wants, she refuses to save her brother's life at the cost of her virginity.

Isabella then goes to the prison to tell her brother the bad news that he will not be reprieved. You may imagine how Claudio feels when she then mentions that there was a way of saving his life, but at such a terrible cost (the loss of her virginity to Angelo) he would not want to agree to it.

The audience finds its sympathies shifting. Is Isabella so good that we admire her for suffering the loss of her brother in order to preserve her own purity? Or do we think she values her own purity too much, and should sacrifice it in order for him to live?

Script

Act II, Scene 2

Angelo's room in the court of justice

SERVANT:	Here is the sister of the man condemn'd Desires access to you.
ANGELO:	Hath he a sister?
PROVOST:	Ay, my good lord; a very virtuous maid, And to be shortly of a sisterhood, If not already.
ANGELO:	Well, let her be admitted.

Exit Servant

Enter Isabella and Lucio

	You're welcome: what's your will?
ISABELLA:	I am a woeful suitor to your honour, Please but your honour hear me.
ANGELO:	Well; what's your suit?
ISABELLA:	There is a vice that most I do abhor, And most desire should meet the blow of justice; For which I would not plead, but that I must; For which I must not plead, but that I am At war 'twixt will and will not.
ANGELO:	Well; the matter?
ISABELLA:	I have a brother is condemn'd to die: I do beseech you, let it be his fault, And not my brother.
ANGELO:	Condemn the fault and not the actor of it? Why, every fault's condemn'd ere it be done: Mine were the very cipher of a function, To fine the faults whose fine stands in record, And let go by the actor.

ISABELLA: O just but severe law!
             I had a brother, then. Heaven keep your honour!

LUCIO: *Aside to Isabella* Give't not o'er so: to him again,
                entreat him;
             Kneel down before him, hang upon his gown:
             You are too cold; if you should need a pin,
             You could not with more tame a tongue desire it:
             To him, I say!

ISABELLA: Must he needs die?

ANGELO: Maiden, no remedy.

ISABELLA: Yes; I do think that you might pardon him,
             And neither heaven nor man grieve at the mercy.

ANGELO: I will not do't.

ISABELLA: But can you, if you would?

ANGELO: Look, what I will not, that I cannot do.

ISABELLA: But might you do't, and do the world no wrong,
             If so your heart were touch'd with that remorse
             As mine is to him?

ANGELO: He's sentenced; 'tis too late.

LUCIO: *Aside to Isabella* You are too cold.

ISABELLA: Too late? why, no; I, that do speak a word,
             May call it back again. Well, believe this,
             No ceremony that to great ones 'longs,
             Not the king's crown, nor the deputed sword,
             The marshal's truncheon, nor the judge's robe,
             Become them with one half so good a grace
             As mercy does.
             If he had been as you and you as he,
             You would have slipt like him; but he, like you,
             Would not have been so stern.

ANGELO: Pray you, be gone.

ISABELLA: I would to heaven I had your potency,
             And you were Isabel! should it then be thus?
             No; I would tell what 'twere to be a judge,
             And what a prisoner.

LUCIO: *Aside to Isabella*
             Ay, touch him; there's the vein.

ANGELO: Your brother is a forfeit of the law,
             And you but waste your words.

ISABELLA: Alas, alas!
             Why, all the souls that were were forfeit once;
             And He that might the vantage best have took

Found out the remedy. How would you be,
If He, which is the top of judgment, should
But judge you as you are? O, think on that;
And mercy then will breathe within your lips,
Like man new made.

ANGELO: Be you content, fair maid;
It is the law, not I condemn your brother:
Were he my kinsman, brother, or my son,
It should be thus with him: he must die tomorrow.

ISABELLA: To-morrow! O, that's sudden! Spare him, spare him!
He's not prepared for death. Even for our kitchens
We kill the fowl of season: shall we serve heaven
With less respect than we do minister
To our gross selves? Good, good my lord, bethink you;
Who is it that hath died for this offence?
There's many have committed it.

LUCIO: *Aside to Isabella* Ay, well said.

ANGELO: The law hath not been dead, though it hath slept:
Those many had not dared to do that evil,
If the first that did the edict infringe
Had answer'd for his deed: now 'tis awake
Takes note of what is done; and, like a prophet,
Looks in a glass, that shows what future evils,
Either new, or by remissness new-conceived,
And so in progress to be hatch'd and born,
Are now to have no successive degrees,
But, ere they live, to end.

ISABELLA: Yet show some pity.

ANGELO: I show it most of all when I show justice;
For then I pity those I do not know,
Which a dismiss'd offence would after gall;
And do him right that, answering one foul wrong,
Lives not to act another. Be satisfied;
Your brother dies to-morrow; be content.

ISABELLA: So you must be the first that gives this sentence,
And he, that suffers. O, it is excellent
To have a giant's strength; but it is tyrannous
To use it like a giant.

LUCIO: *Aside to Isabella* That's well said.

ISABELLA: Could great men thunder
As Jove himself does, Jove would ne'er be quiet,
For every pelting, petty officer
Would use his heaven for thunder;
Nothing but thunder! Merciful Heaven,

A dramatic moment from the 1991 performance of 'Measure for Measure'.

Thou rather with thy sharp and sulphurous bolt
Split'st the unwedgeable and gnarled oak
Than the soft myrtle: but man, proud man,
Drest in a little brief authority,
Most ignorant of what he's most assured,
His glassy essence, like an angry ape,
Plays such fantastic tricks before high heaven
As make the angels weep.

LUCIO: *Aside to Isabella* O, to him, to him, wench! he will relent;
He's coming; I perceive 't.

ISABELLA: We cannot weigh our brother with ourself:
Great men may jest with saints; 'tis wit in them,
But in the less foul profanation.

LUCIO: Thou'rt i' the right, girl; more o' that.

ISABELLA: That in the captain's but a choleric word,
Which in the soldier is flat blasphemy.

LUCIO: *Aside to Isabella* Art avised o' that? more on't.

ANGELO: Why do you put these sayings upon me?

ISABELLA: Because authority, though it err like others,
Hath yet a kind of medicine in itself,
That skins the vice o' the top. Go to your bosom;
Knock there, and ask your heart what it doth know
That's like my brother's fault: if it confess
A natural guiltiness such as is his,
Let it not sound a thought upon your tongue
Against my brother's life.

ANGELO: *Aside* She speaks, and 'tis
Such sense, that my sense breeds with it. Fare you well.

ISABELLA: Gentle my lord, turn back.

ANGELO: I will bethink me: come again tomorrow.

ISABELLA: Hark how I'll bribe you: good my lord, turn back.

ANGELO: How! bribe me?

ISABELLA: Ay, with such gifts that heaven shall share with you.

LUCIO: *Aside to Isabella* You had marr'd all else.

ISABELLA: Not with fond shekels of the tested gold,
Or stones whose rates are either rich or poor
As fancy values them; but with true prayers
That shall be up at heaven and enter there
Ere sun-rise, prayers from preserved souls,
From fasting maids whose minds are dedicate
To nothing temporal.

ANGELO: Well; come to me to-morrow.

LUCIO:	*Aside to Isabella* Go to; 'tis well; away!
ISABELLA:	Heaven keep your honour safe!
ANGELO:	*Aside* Amen: For I am that way going to temptation, Where prayers cross.
ISABELLA:	At what hour to-morrow Shall I attend your lordship?
ANGELO:	At any time 'fore noon.
ISABELLA:	'Save your honour!

Exeunt Isabella, Lucio, and Provost

ANGELO:	From thee, even from thy virtue! What's this, what's this? Is this her fault or mine? The tempter or the tempted, who sins most? Ha! Can it be That modesty may more betray our sense Than woman's lightness? Having waste ground enough, Shall we desire to raze the sanctuary And pitch our evils there? O, fie, fie, fie! What dost thou, or what art thou, Angelo? Dost thou desire her foully for those things That make her good? O, let her brother live! Thieves for their robbery have authority When judges steal themselves. What, do I love her, That I desire to hear her speak again, And feast upon her eyes? What is't I dream on? Never could the strumpet, With all her double vigour, art and nature, Once stir my temper; but this virtuous maid Subdues me quite. Ever till now, When men were fond, I smiled and wonder'd how.

Exit

Act II, Scene 4

A room in Angelo's house

Enter Angelo

ANGELO:	When I would pray and think, I think and pray To several subjects. Heaven hath my empty words; Whilst my invention, hearing not my tongue, Anchors on Isabel: Heaven in my mouth, As if I did but only chew his name; And in my heart the strong and swelling evil Of my conception.

Enter a Servant

	How now! who's there?
SERVANT:	One Isabel, a sister, desires access to you.
ANGELO:	Teach her the way.

Exit Servant

O heavens!
Why does my blood thus muster to my heart,
Making both it unable for itself,
And dispossessing all my other parts
Of necessary fitness?

Enter Isabella

How now, fair maid?

ISABELLA: I am come to know your pleasure.

ANGELO: That you might know it, would much better please me
Than to demand what 'tis. Your brother cannot live.

ISABELLA: Even so. Heaven keep your honour!

ANGELO: Yet may he live awhile; and, it may be,
As long as you or I: yet he must die.

ISABELLA: Under your sentence?

ANGELO: Yea.

ISABELLA: When, I beseech you? that in his reprieve,
Longer or shorter, he may be so fitted
That his soul sicken not.

ANGELO: Say you so? then I shall pose you quickly.
Which had you rather, that the most just law
Now took your brother's life; or, to redeem him,
Give up your body to such sweet uncleanness
As she that he hath stain'd?

ISABELLA: Sir, believe this,
I had rather give my body than my soul.

ANGELO: I talk not of your soul. Answer to this:
I, now the voice of the recorded law,
Pronounce a sentence on your brother's life:
Might there not be a charity in sin
To save this brother's life?

ISABELLA: Please you to do't,
I'll take it as a peril to my soul,
It is no sin at all, but charity.

ANGELO: Pleased you to do't at peril of your soul,
Were equal poise of sin and charity.

ISABELLA: That I do beg his life, if it be sin,
Heaven let me bear it; you granting of my suit,

If that be sin, I'll make it my morn prayer
To have it added to the faults of mine,
And nothing of your answer.

ANGELO: Nay, but hear me.
Your sense pursues not mine: either you are ignorant,
Or seem so craftily; and that's not good.

ISABELLA: Let me be ignorant, and in nothing good,
But graciously to know I am no better.

ANGELO: But mark me;
To be received plain, I'll speak more gross:
Your brother is to die.

ISABELLA: So.

ANGELO: Admit no other way to save his life, –
But that you, his sister,
Finding yourself desired of such a person,
Whose credit with the judge, or own great place,
Could fetch your brother from the manacles
Of the all-binding law; and that there were
No earthly mean to save him, but that either
You must lay down the treasures of your body
To this supposed, or else to let him suffer;
What would you do?

ISABELLA: As much for my poor brother as myself:
That is, were I under the terms of death,
The impression of keen whips I'ld wear as rubies,
Ere I would yield my body up to shame.

ANGELO: Then must your brother die.

ISABELLA: And 'twere the cheaper way:
Better it were a brother died at once,
Than that a sister, by redeeming him,
Should die for ever.

ANGELO: Were not you then as cruel as the sentence
That you have slander'ed so?
You seem'd of late to make the law a tyrant;
And rather proved the sliding of your brother
A merriment than a vice.

ISABELLA: O, pardon me, my lord; it oft falls out,
To have what we would have, we speak not what we mean.

ANGELO: We are all frail.

ISABELLA: Else let my brother die,
If not a feodary, but only he
Owe and succeed thy weakness.

ANGELO: Nay, women are frail too.

ISABELLA: Ay, as the glasses where they view themselves;
Which are as easy broke as they make forms.
Women! Help Heaven! men their creation mar
In profiting by them. Nay, call us ten times frail;
For we are soft as our complexions are,
And credulous to false prints.

ANGELO: I think it well:
And from this testimony of your own sex, – let me be bold;
I do arrest your words. Be that you are,
That is, a woman, as you are well express'd
By all external warrants, show it now.
Plainly conceive, I love you.

ISABELLA: My brother did love Juliet,
And you tell me that he shall die for it.

ANGELO: He shall not, Isabel, if you give me love.

ISABELLA: I know your virtue hath a licence in't,
Which seems a little fouler than it is,
To pluck on others.

ANGELO: Believe me, on mine honour,
My words express my purpose.

ISABELLA: Ha! little honour to be much believed,
And most pernicious purpose! Seeming, seeming!
I will proclaim thee, Angelo; look for't:
Sign me a present pardon for my brother,
Or with an outstretch'd throat I'll tell the world aloud
What man thou art.

ANGELO: Who will believe thee, Isabel?
My unsoil'd name, the austereness of my life,
My vouch against you, and my place i' the state,
Will so your accusation overweigh,
That you shall stifle in your own report
And smell of calumny. I have begun,
And now I give my sensual race the rein:
Fit thy consent to my sharp appetite;
Lay by all nicety and prolixious blushes,
That banish what they sue for; redeem thy brother
By yielding up thy body to my will;
Or else he must not only die the death,
But thy unkindness shall his death draw out
To lingering sufferance. Answer me to-morrow,
Or, by the affection that now guides me most,
        I'll prove a tyrant to him. As for you,
    Say what you can, my false o'erweighs your true.

Exit

ISABELLA: To whom should I complain? Did I tell this,
Who would believe me? I'll to my brother:
Though he hath fallen by prompture of the blood,
Yet hath he in him such a mind of honour.
That, had he twenty heads to tender down
On twenty bloody blocks, he'ld yield them up,
Before his sister should her body stoop
To such abhorr'd pollution.
Then, Isabel, live chaste, and, brother, die:
More than our brother is our chastity.
I'll tell him yet of Angelo's request,
And fit his mind to death, for his soul's rest.

Exit

Act III, Scene 1

In the Prison

Enter Isabella

ISABELLA: My business is a word or two with Claudio.

PROVOST: And very welcome. Look, signior, here's your sister.

CLAUDIO: Now, sister, what's the comfort?

ISABELLA: Why,
As all comforts are; most good, most good indeed.
Lord Angelo, having affairs to heaven,
Intends you for his swift ambassador,
Where you shall be an everlasting leiger:
Therefore your best appointment make with speed;
To-morrow you set on.

CLAUDIO: Is there no remedy?

ISABELLA: None, but such remedy as, to save a head,
To cleave a heart in twain.

CLAUDIO: But is there any?

ISABELLA: Yes, brother, you may live:
There is a devilish mercy in the judge,
If you'll implore it, that will free your life,
But fetter you till death.

CLAUDIO: Perpetual durance?

ISABELLA: Ay, just; perpetual durance, a restraint,
Though all the world's vastidity you had,
To a determine scope.

CLAUDIO: But in what nature?

ISABELLA: In such a one as, you consenting to't,
Would bark your honour from that trunk you bear,
And leave you naked.

CLAUDIO: Let me know the point.

ISABELLA: O, I do fear thee, Claudio; and I quake,
Lest thou a feverous life shouldst entertain,
And six or seven winters more respect
Than a perpetual honour. Darest thou die?

CLAUDIO: If I must die,
I will encounter darkness as a bride,
And hug it in mine arms.

ISABELLA: There spake my brother; there my father's grave
Did utter forth a voice. Yes, thou must die:
Thou art too noble to conserve a life
In base appliances. Dost thou think, Claudio?
If I would yield him my virginity,
Thou mightst be freed.

CLAUDIO: O heavens! it cannot be.

ISABELLA: Yes, he would give't thee, from this rank offence,
So to offend him still. This night's the time
That I should do what I abhor to name,
Or else thou diest to-morrow.

CLAUDIO: Thou shalt not do't.

ISABELLA: O, were it but my life,
I'ld throw it down for your deliverance
As frankly as a pin.

CLAUDIO: Thanks, dear Isabel.

ISABELLA: Be ready, Claudio, for your death tomorrow.

CLAUDIO: Death is a fearful thing.

ISABELLA: And shamed life a hateful.

CLAUDIO: Ay, but to die, and go we know not where;
To lie in cold obstruction and to rot;
This sensible warm motion to become
A kneaded clod; and the delighted spirit
To bathe in fiery floods, or to reside
In thrilling region of thick-ribbed ice;
To be imprison'd in the viewless winds,
And blown with restless violence round about
The pendent world; or to be worse than worst
Of those that lawless and incertain thought
Imagine howling: 'tis too horrible!
The weariest and most loathed worldly life
That age, ache, penury and imprisonment
Can lay on nature is a paradise
To what we fear of death.

ISABELLA: Alas, alas!

CLAUDIO:	Sweet sister, let me live:
	What sin you do to save a brother's life,
	Nature dispenses with the deed so far
	That it becomes a virtue.
ISABELLA:	O you beast!
	O faithless coward! O dishonest wretch!
	Wilt thou be made a man out of my vice?
	Is't not a kind of incest, to take life
	From thine own sister's shame? What should I think?
	I'll pray a thousand prayers for thy death,
	No word to save thee.
CLAUDIO:	Nay, hear me, Isabel.
ISABELLA:	O, fie, fie, fie!
	'Tis best thou diest quickly.
CLAUDIO:	O hear me, Isabella!

Postscript

Purpose
- to create dramatic tension and suspense
- to explore morality and principle

Effects
- conflicting sympathies as the situation develops
- sympathy with Isabella as she is trapped
- sympathy with Claudio as his death seems inevitable
- sympathy with Angelo as he admits his own weakness

Devices
- dramatic struggle within Isabella's mind
- dramatic struggle within Angelo's mind
- dramatic struggle between Angelo and Isabella
- irony
- aside
- Lucio's third-party commentary and participation

Glossary

sisterhood	convent of nuns
suit	case brought before a court
abhor	despise
cipher	insignificant number or figure
entreat	beg
potency	power, authority
forfeit	loss as a punishment or penalty
edict	law, order
infringe	to break a rule

remissness	forgetfulness, neglect
gall	injure
myrtle	a plant with fragrant white flowers
profanation	disrespect
choleric	bad-tempered
marr'd	spoiled
shekels	money
temporal	here and now
raze	demolish
muster	assemble like an army
feodary	someone who inherits
licence	allowance, freedom
calumny	malicious gossip or lies
prolixious	time-wasting
leiger	ambassador
fetter	keep in chains
durance	confinement
vastidity	immenseness, hugeness
pendent	hanging in space
penury	poverty

Close-up on language

1 Which words does Angelo use to show that he is busy?

2 Which words does he use to reinforce the authority and the law?

3 Which words does Isabella use to reinforce the idea of tenderness and mercy?

4 Which words have the effect of showing that Angelo is beginning to be less sure of himself?

Understanding character

Try to get inside Isabella's mind. When she says "Spare him, spare him!", what she says is what she feels – a desperate wish for Angelo to be merciful. On the other hand, when she says "Even so. Heaven keep your honour!" she feels more than she says. She is determined not to be emotional, and is struggling to keep herself under control in the face of this powerful man. The news that her brother must die would not make her feel kindly towards Angelo, but she is restraining her feelings at this point. Think about other moments where a character's thoughts and feelings may not be quite the same as what is said.

1 What is in Isabella's mind at these points?

> "I am
> At war 'twixt will and will not"

"O just but severe law!
I had a brother, then."

"it is excellent
To have a giant's strength; but it is tyrannous
To use it like a giant."

2 What is in Angelo's mind at these points?

"Look, what I will not, that I cannot do."

"Pray you, be gone."

"Why do you put these sayings upon me?"

"She speaks, and 'tis
Such sense, that my sense breeds with it."

"How! bribe me?"

3 What is Lucio thinking and feeling at these points?

"if you should need a pin,
You could not with more tame a tongue desire it"

"You are too cold."

"Thou'rt i' the right, girl; more o' that."

Personal response

1 Do you think Angelo is any, none or some of the following?
   - a ruthless exploiter of an innocent young woman
   - a man trying to live by high standards but weakened by falling in love
   - a hypocrite who uses his power for his own sexual advantage
   - a man who is learning that the Law is less important than mercy
   - a man who is learning that you have to rule yourself before you try to rule over other people

2 What would you say to Isabella if you were Claudio?

3 How do you feel about Isabella when she realises that Angelo will deny all this?

4 How do you feel about Isabella when she tells her brother she cannot agree to sparing his life at the cost of her own virginity?

Understanding performance

Staging and directing

1 What could costume and props add to the effect of the opening scene? Think of clothes that suggest authority for Angelo, and objects on his desk.

2 What should the actor playing Angelo do at these points?

> "Well; the matter?"
>
> "He's sentenced; 'tis too late."
>
> "Pray you, be gone."
>
> "I will bethink me: come again tomorrow."
>
> "When I would pray and think, I think and pray
> To several subjects. Heaven hath my empty words"

3 What should the actor playing Isabella do at these points?

> "Heaven keep your honour!"
>
> "I would to heaven I had your potency,
> And you were Isabel!"
>
> "'Save your honour!" *Exit*

4 What could the actor playing Lucio do if he stood in the following positions?
  - behind Angelo, facing Isabella
  - at the side where neither could see him

Practical work

Solo or in pairs

1 Read the line "Look, what I will not, that I cannot do", exaggerating the tone of:
  - explaining politely
  - answering crossly.

  Which is better?

  Read the line again, emphasising the two uses of the word "I".

  Read the line again, emphasising the words "will" and "cannot".

  Read the line again, emphasising the word "what" and then read it again, emphasising the word "that".

  What differences are created by changing the emphasis?

  What advice will you give the actor about the tone and the emphasis of this line?

2 Read the line "Gentle my lord, turn back", with:
  - a begging, desperate tone
  - a calm, reasoning tone.

  Which do you think is better?

3 Read the line "How! bribe me?" as:
  - a question showing interest
  - an angry response to someone daring to think he can be bribed.

  Which do you think is better?

4 Read the line "Even so. Heaven keep your honour!" to suggest:

- bravely accepting the verdict
- disappointment
- bitterness and anger.

Which do you think is best?

5 Read the lines

"Yet may he live awhile; and, it may be,
As long as you or I: yet he must die"

suggesting, by pauses and emphasis that Angelo is:

- changing his mind, and then recovers himself
- weighing this up in his own mind.

Which do you think is better?

6 Design a theatre poster or video cover showing Isabella begging the Duke to be merciful. Use details of clothing, setting and props to suggest authority, religion and family affection.

7 Imagine Isabella wrote to a magazine agony-aunt explaining her problem. What, if you were replying, would you tell her?

In groups

1 Hot seat

a Put Claudio in the hot seat and ask him how he felt about his sister's refusal to do what Angelo wanted in order to save his life.

b Put Isabella in the hot seat and ask her what she thinks of Angelo, and what she would be prepared to do to save her brother's life.

c Put Angelo in the hot seat and question him about his feelings for Isabella and whether he is fit to judge other people for failings that he shares.

2 Tableau talkback

The group freezes in a tableau of the scene in Angelo's office. The questioner walks around the three figures in the tableau and asks what different characters think about the situation and each other.

3 Perform the section where Lucio tries to make Isabella more persuasive.

4 Perform the section where Isabella begins to make Angelo change his mind.

Social, cultural and historical aspects

1 What does this episode tell an audience about religious belief, moral attitudes and laws different from our own?

2 Why may a modern audience take a different view of Isabella?

3 How would you advertise the play so that it was relevant and interesting to a modern audience?

8

How to do it – from *Julius Caesar*

Introduction

*J*ulius Caesar, Emperor of Rome, has been murdered by a group led by Brutus. Brutus was a very fair-minded man who did not want to see Caesar killed, but he thought it was the only way to stop him becoming a dictator.

Mark Antony was close to Julius Caesar, and some of Brutus's friends thought that he should have been killed too, but Brutus didn't want more bloodshed.

Brutus decides to let Mark Antony speak to the Roman people at Caesar's funeral. He wants to show himself to be a fair man who trusts the public to understand the truth.

Mark Antony quickly accepts the offer of speaking, seeing a chance to use the situation against the killers of his friend.

Sir John Gielgud in 'Julius Caesar' at the National Theatre, 1977.

Script

Act III, Scene 1

In the capitol, alone, left with Caesar's corpse

ANTONY:　　O, pardon me, thou bleeding piece of earth,
　　　　　That I am meek and gentle with these butchers!
　　　　　Thou art the ruins of the noblest man
　　　　　That ever lived in the tide of times.
　　　　　Woe to the hands that shed this costly blood!
　　　　　Over thy wounds now do I prophesy, –
　　　　　Which, like dumb mouths, do ope their ruby lips,
　　　　　To beg the voice and utterance of my tongue –
　　　　　A curse shall light upon the limbs of men;
　　　　　Domestic fury and fierce civil strife
　　　　　Shall cumber all the parts of Italy;
　　　　　Blood and destruction shall be so in use
　　　　　And dreadful objects so familiar
　　　　　That mothers shall but smile when they behold
　　　　　Their infants quarter'd with the hands of war;
　　　　　All pity choked with custom of fell deeds:
　　　　　And Caesar's spirit, ranging for revenge,
　　　　　Shall in these confines with a monarch's voice
　　　　　Cry 'Havoc,' and let slip the dogs of war;
　　　　　That this foul deed shall smell above the earth
　　　　　With carrion men, groaning for burial.

Act III, Scene 2

The Forum

Enter Brutus and Cassius, and a throng of Citizens

CITIZENS:　　We will be satisfied; let us be satisfied.

BRUTUS:　　Then follow me, and give me audience, friends.
　　　　　Those that will hear me speak, let 'em stay here;
　　　　　And public reasons shall be rendered
　　　　　Of Caesar's death.

FIRST CITIZEN:　　I will hear Brutus speak.

SECOND CITIZEN:　　The noble Brutus is ascended: silence!

BRUTUS:　　Be patient till the last.
　　　　　Romans, countrymen, and lovers! hear me for my
　　　　　cause, and be silent, that you may hear: believe me
　　　　　for mine honour, and have respect to mine honour, that
　　　　　you may believe: censure me in your wisdom, and
　　　　　awake your senses, that you may the better judge.

If there be any in this assembly, any dear friend of
Caesar's, to him I say, that Brutus' love to Caesar
was no less than his. If then that friend demand
why Brutus rose against Caesar, this is my answer:
– Not that I loved Caesar less, but that I loved
Rome more. Had you rather Caesar were living and
die all slaves, than that Caesar were dead, to live
all free men? As Caesar loved me, I weep for him;
as he was fortunate, I rejoice at it; as he was
valiant, I honour him: but, as he was ambitious, I
slew him. There is tears for his love; joy for his
fortune; honour for his valour; and death for his
ambition. Who is here so base that would be a
bondman? If any, speak; for him have I offended.
Who is here so rude that would not be a Roman? If
any, speak; for him have I offended. Who is here so
vile that will not love his country? If any, speak;
for him have I offended. I pause for a reply.

ALL: None, Brutus, none.

BRUTUS: Then none have I offended. I have done no more to
Caesar than you shall do to Brutus. The question of
his death is enrolled in the Capitol; his glory not
extenuated, wherein he was worthy, nor his offences
enforced, for which he suffered death.

Enter Antony and others, with Caesar's body

Here comes his body, mourned by Mark Antony: who,
though he had no hand in his death, shall receive
the benefit of his dying, a place in the
commonwealth; as which of you shall not? With this
I depart, – that, as I slew my best lover for the
good of Rome, I have the same dagger for myself,
when it shall please my country to need my death.

ALL: Live, Brutus! live, live!

FIRST CITIZEN: Bring him with triumph home unto his house.

SECOND CITIZEN: Give him a statue with his ancestors.

THIRD CITIZEN: Let him be Caesar.

FOURTH CITIZEN: Caesar's better parts shall be crown'd in Brutus.

FIRST CITIZEN: We'll bring him to his house with shouts and clamours.

BRUTUS: My countrymen,—

SECOND CITIZEN: Peace, silence! Brutus speaks.

FIRST CITIZEN: Peace, ho!

BRUTUS: Good countrymen, let me depart alone,
And, for my sake, stay here with Antony:

Do grace to Caesar's corpse, and grace his speech
Tending to Caesar's glories; which Mark Antony,
By our permission, is allow'd to make.
I do entreat you, not a man depart,
Save I alone, till Antony have spoke.

Exit

FIRST CITIZEN:　Stay, ho! and let us hear Mark Antony.

THIRD CITIZEN:　Let him go up into the public chair;
We'll hear him. Noble Antony, go up.

ANTONY:　For Brutus' sake, I am beholding to you.

Goes into the pulpit

FOURTH CITIZEN:　What does he say of Brutus?

THIRD CITIZEN:　He says, for Brutus' sake,
He finds himself beholding to us all.

FOURTH CITIZEN:　'Twere best he speak no harm of Brutus here.

FIRST CITIZEN:　This Caesar was a tyrant.

THIRD CITIZEN:　Nay, that's certain:
We are blest that Rome is rid of him.

SECOND CITIZEN:　Peace! let us hear what Antony can say.

ANTONY:　You gentle Romans,—

CITIZENS:　Peace, ho! let us hear him.

ANTONY:　Friends, Romans, countrymen, lend me your ears;
I come to bury Caesar, not to praise him.
The evil that men do lives after them;
The good is oft interred with their bones;
So let it be with Caesar. The noble Brutus
Hath told you Caesar was ambitious:
If it were so, it was a grievous fault,
And grievously hath Caesar answer'd it.
Here, under leave of Brutus and the rest –
For Brutus is an honourable man;
So are they all, all honourable men –
Come I to speak in Caesar's funeral.
He was my friend, faithful and just to me:
But Brutus says he was ambitious;
And Brutus is an honourable man.
He hath brought many captives home to Rome
Whose ransoms did the general coffers fill:
Did this in Caesar seem ambitious?
When that the poor have cried, Caesar hath wept:
Ambition should be made of sterner stuff:
Yet Brutus says he was ambitious;
And Brutus is an honourable man.

You all did see that on the Lupercal
I thrice presented him a kingly crown,
Which he did thrice refuse: was this ambition?
Yet Brutus says he was ambitious;
And, sure, he is an honourable man.
I speak not to disprove what Brutus spoke,
But here I am to speak what I do know.
You all did love him once, not without cause:
What cause withholds you then, to mourn for him?
O judgment! thou art fled to brutish beasts,
And men have lost their reason. Bear with me;
My heart is in the coffin there with Caesar,
And I must pause till it come back to me.

FIRST CITIZEN: Methinks there is much reason in his sayings.

SECOND CITIZEN: If thou consider rightly of the matter,
Caesar has had great wrong.

THIRD CITIZEN: Has he, masters?
I fear there will a worse come in his place.

FOURTH CITIZEN: Mark'd ye his words? He would not take the crown;
Therefore 'tis certain he was not ambitious.

FIRST CITIZEN: If it be found so, some will dear abide it.

SECOND CITIZEN: Poor soul! his eyes are red as fire with weeping.

THIRD CITIZEN: There's not a nobler man in Rome than Antony.

FOURTH CITIZEN: Now mark him, he begins again to speak.

ANTONY: But yesterday the word of Caesar might
Have stood against the world; now lies he there.
And none so poor to do him reverence.
O masters, if I were disposed to stir
Your hearts and minds to mutiny and rage,
I should do Brutus wrong, and Cassius wrong,
Who, you all know, are honourable men:
I will not do them wrong; I rather choose
To wrong the dead, to wrong myself and you,
Than I will wrong such honourable men.
But here's a parchment with the seal of Caesar;
I found it in his closet, 'tis his will:
Let but the commons hear this testament –
Which, pardon me, I do not mean to read –
And they would go and kiss dead Caesar's wounds
And dip their napkins in his sacred blood,
Yea, beg a hair of him for memory,
And, dying, mention it within their wills,
Bequeathing it as a rich legacy
Unto their issue.

A watercolour from 1815 shows Charles Mayne Young as Cassius in 'Julius Caesar'.

FOURTH CITIZEN:	We'll hear the will: read it, Mark Antony.
ALL:	The will, the will! we will hear Caesar's will.
ANTONY:	Have patience, gentle friends, I must not read it;
	It is not meet you know how Caesar loved you.
	You are not wood, you are not stones, but men;
	And, being men, bearing the will of Caesar,
	It will inflame you, it will make you mad:
	'Tis good you know not that you are his heirs;
	For, if you should, O, what would come of it!
FOURTH CITIZEN:	Read the will; we'll hear it, Antony;
	You shall read us the will, Caesar's will.
ANTONY:	Will you be patient? will you stay awhile?
	I have o'ershot myself to tell you of it:
	I fear I wrong the honourable men
	Whose daggers have stabb'd Caesar; I do fear it.
FOURTH CITIZEN:	They were traitors: honourable men!
ALL:	The will! the testament!
SECOND CITIZEN:	They were villains, murderers: the will! read the will.
ANTONY:	You will compel me, then, to read the will?
	Then make a ring about the corpse of Caesar,
	And let me show you him that made the will.
	Shall I descend? and will you give me leave?
SEVERAL CITIZENS:	Come down.
SECOND CITIZEN:	Descend.
THIRD CITIZEN:	You shall have leave.

Antony comes down

FOURTH CITIZEN:	A ring; stand round.
FIRST CITIZEN:	Stand from the hearse, stand from the body.
SECOND CITIZEN:	Room for Antony, most noble Antony.
ANTONY:	Nay, press not so upon me; stand far off.
SEVERAL CITIZENS:	Stand back; room; bear back.
ANTONY:	If you have tears, prepare to shed them now.
	You all do know this mantle: I remember
	The first time ever Caesar put it on;
	'Twas on a summer's evening, in his tent,
	That day he overcame the Nervii:
	Look, in this place ran Cassius' dagger through:
	See what a rent the envious Casca made:
	Through this the well-beloved Brutus stabb'd;
	And as he pluck'd his cursed steel away,
	Mark how the blood of Caesar follow'd it,

As rushing out of doors, to be resolved
If Brutus so unkindly knock'd, or no;
For Brutus, as you know, was Caesar's angel:
Judge, O you gods, how dearly Caesar loved him!
This was the most unkindest cut of all;
For when the noble Caesar saw him stab,
Ingratitude, more strong than traitors' arms,
Quite vanquish'd him: then burst his mighty heart;
And, in his mantle muffling up his face,
Even at the base of Pompey's statua,
Which all the while ran blood, great Caesar fell.
O, what a fall was there, my countrymen!
Then I, and you, and all of us fell down,
Whilst bloody treason flourish'd over us.
O, now you weep; and, I perceive, you feel
The dint of pity: these are gracious drops.
Kind souls, what, weep you when you but behold
Our Caesar's vesture wounded? Look you here,
Here is himself, marr'd, as you see, with traitors.

FIRST CITIZEN:	O piteous spectacle!
SECOND CITIZEN:	O noble Caesar!
THIRD CITIZEN:	O woful day!
FOURTH CITIZEN:	O traitors, villains!
FIRST CITIZEN:	O most bloody sight!
SECOND CITIZEN:	We will be revenged.
ALL:	Revenge! About! Seek! Burn! Fire! Kill! Slay! Let not a traitor live!
ANTONY:	Stay, countrymen.
FIRST CITIZEN:	Peace there! hear the noble Antony.
SECOND CITIZEN:	We'll hear him, we'll follow him, we'll die with him.
ANTONY:	Good friends, sweet friends, let me not stir you up

To such a sudden flood of mutiny.
They that have done this deed are honourable:
What private griefs they have, alas, I know not,
That made them do it: they are wise and honourable,
And will, no doubt, with reasons answer you.
I come not, friends, to steal away your hearts:
I am no orator, as Brutus is;
But, as you know me all, a plain blunt man,
That love my friend; and that they know full well
That gave me public leave to speak of him:
For I have neither wit, nor words, nor worth,
Action, nor utterance, nor the power of speech,

To stir men's blood: I only speak right on;
I tell you that which you yourselves do know,
Show you sweet Caesar's wounds, poor poor dumb mouths,
And bid them speak for me: but were I Brutus,
And Brutus Antony, there were an Antony
Would ruffle up your spirits and put a tongue
In every wound of Caesar that should move
The stones of Rome to rise and mutiny.

ALL: We'll mutiny.

FIRST CITIZEN: We'll burn the house of Brutus.

THIRD CITIZEN: Away, then! come, seek the conspirators.

ANTONY: Yet hear me, countrymen; yet hear me speak.

ALL: Peace, ho! Hear Antony. Most noble Antony!

ANTONY: Why, friends, you go to do you know not what:
                        Wherein hath Caesar thus deserved your loves?
                        Alas, you know not: I must tell you then:
                        You have forgot the will I told you of.

ALL: Most true. The will! Let's stay and hear the will.

ANTONY: Here is the will, and under Caesar's seal.
                        To every Roman citizen he gives,
                        To every several man, seventy-five drachmas.

SECOND CITIZEN: Most noble Caesar! We'll revenge his death.

THIRD CITIZEN: O royal Caesar!

ANTONY: Hear me with patience.

ALL: Peace, ho!

ANTONY: Moreover, he hath left you all his walks,
                        His private arbours and new-planted orchards,
                        On this side Tiber; he hath left them you,
                        And to your heirs for ever, common pleasures,
                        To walk abroad, and recreate yourselves.
                        Here was a Caesar! when comes such another?

FIRST CITIZEN: Never, never. Come, away, away!
                        We'll burn his body in the holy place,
                        And with the brands fire the traitors' houses.
                        Take up the body.

SECOND CITIZEN: Go fetch fire.

THIRD CITIZEN: Pluck down benches.

FOURTH CITIZEN: Pluck down forms, windows, anything.

Exeunt Citizens with the body

ANTONY: Now let it work. Mischief, thou art afoot,
                        Take thou what course thou wilt!

Postscript

Purpose
- to illustrate great historical events
- to show the effects of speech on people
- to show that openness and honesty are not always the best way to influence people

Effects
- changing view of Mark Antony
- changing view of the ordinary people (plebeians or plebs)

Devices
- contrast between Brutus and Mark Antony
- changing sympathies of the people
- Mark Antony's indirect stirring up of the crowd
- Mark Antony's gradual undermining of Brutus's reputation
- rhetoric

Glossary

cumber	distress
fell	savage
censure	judge
bondman	slave
rude	ignorant
extenuated	underrated
entreat	beg
beholding	obliged
interred	buried
coffers	money chests
Lupercal	public holiday ceremony
Cassius	one of the conspirators who joined Brutus in the killing
bequeathing	leaving in a will
issue	children and grandchildren
meet	appropriate
hearse	framework for a coffin
mantle	cloak
Nervii	enemies of Rome
Casca	another of the conspirators who joined Brutus in the killing
vesture	clothes
marr'd	destroyed
arbours	ornamental gardens
recreate	relax and restore

Close-up on language

1 Which words does Antony choose to make himself seem ordinary and humble?

2 Which words does he choose to make himself seem innocent of any motives?

3 Which words have the effect of planting ideas of rebellion in his listeners' minds?

4 Which words reveal that he planned to create violence from the start?

5 Which words show his satisfaction with the way things have turned out?

Understanding character

Getting into thoughts and feelings

When Mark Antony says "pardon me (…) That I am meek and gentle with these butchers!", what he says is what he feels – that it is a shame to seem so unmoved. On the other hand, when he says he cannot go on because "My heart is in the coffin there with Caesar" he may actually be very much in control of himself. He may be saying it to gain sympathy, rather than be unable to go on. His thoughts and feelings may have more to do with manipulating the crowd's feelings than with his own feelings.

1 What is in Brutus's mind at these points?

> "censure me in your wisdom"
>
> "Not that I loved Caesar less, but that I loved Rome more."
>
> "tears for his love; joy for his fortune; honour for his valour; and death for his ambition."

2 What is in Mark Antony's mind at these points?

> | | "Thou art the ruins of the noblest man
That ever lived in the tide of times." |
> |---|---|
> | THIRD CITIZEN: | "Let him be Caesar." (of Brutus) |
> | BRUTUS: | "not a man depart,
Save I alone, till Antony have spoke." |
> | FOURTH CITIZEN: | "'Twere best he speak no harm of Brutus here." |
> | SECOND CITIZEN: | "Poor soul! his eyes are red as fire with weeping." |

3 What is each citizen thinking and feeling at these points in Mark Antony's speech?

> "He hath brought many captives home to Rome
> Whose ransoms did the general coffers fill"
>
> "When that the poor have cried, Caesar hath wept."
>
> "My heart is in the coffin there with Caesar
> And I must pause till it come back to me."

Personal response

1 What do you think about Brutus's very fair and decent behaviour in letting Mark Antony speak after him when he has left?

2 What do you think was Mark Antony's motive in saying he could not go on because his heart was in the coffin with Caesar?

3 What do you feel about the way the people change in the course of this speech?

Understanding performance

Staging and directing

1 What could costume and props add to the effect of this scene? Think about:
   - the sort of clothes Mark Antony might wear for the funeral speech
   - the sort of mantle that would be needed for Caesar
   - the kind of coffin that might be used
   - whether Caesar's body should be visible on the stage.

2 What should the actor playing Brutus do at these points?

> "be silent, that you may hear"
>
> "By our permission, is allow'd to make"

3 What should the actor playing Mark Antony do at these points?

> "You gentle Romans"
>
> "And Brutus is an honourable man."
>
> "My heart is in the coffin there with Caesar"
>
> "But here's a parchment with the seal of Caesar;
> (…) tis his will (…)
> Which, pardon me, I do not mean to read"
>
> "You all do know this mantle"
>
> "Through this the well-loved Brutus stabb'd"
>
> "Look you here,
> Here is himself, marr'd, as you see, with traitors."

4 What reactions should be shown by the actors listening at these points?

> "We'll bring him to his house with shouts and clamours."
>
> ANTONY: "Look, in this place ran Cassius' dagger through"
>
> ANTONY: "marr'd, as you see, with traitors."

Practical work

Solo or in pairs

1 Read the start of the speech that begins "Friends, Romans, countrymen", with a tone of:

- confidently commanding attention
- cautiously begging for attention.

Which is better?

Try the opening line in the following different orders:

- Romans, countrymen, friends
- Countrymen, Romans, friends.

Try it with a pause after "Friends".

What makes the line an effective start to a speech in front of a hostile audience?

2 Read the line "And Brutus is an honourable man":

- emphasising the word "Brutus"
- emphasising the word "honourable".

3 Design a theatre poster or video cover showing Mark Antony displaying the holes in the mantle of Caesar to the plebs all around him.

In groups

1 Hot seat

a Put Mark Antony in the hot seat and ask him why he planned his revenge on Brutus and how he managed to make the Roman people mutiny.

b Put one of the citizens in the hot seat and question him/her about events in the forum that day.

2 Tableau talkback

The group freezes in a tableau of the scene at three particular stages. The questioner walks around the figures in the tableau and asks what different characters think about the situation.

3 Perform the crowd responses at three stages of Antony's speech, bringing out the change in their feelings towards Antony and Brutus.

Social, cultural and historical aspects

1 What does this episode tell an audience about Shakespeare's view of the public?

2 What events in our society and in our time could be seen as similar to the way in which public opinion is worked on by Mark Antony?

'From a Jack to a King' 1993. This shows the three witches. The musical was based on 'Macbeth'.

How not to do it – from *Coriolanus*

Introduction

Caius Martius, named Coriolanus after his famous conquest of Corioli, has been persuaded to stand as a candidate for the post of Consul in Rome. This is an elected post, so he has to gain the confidence of the Senate and the approval of the Roman people. Unfortunately, he thinks that the ordinary people (the plebeians or plebs) are worthless cowards who should be grateful to him for winning battles for Rome. He cannot bear the thought that he should try to please them so that they vote for him. His supporters try to make him hide his real feelings and put on a false show in order to make the plebs think he respects them.

The audience can admire Coriolanus's honesty in not wanting to hide his real feelings, and can also disapprove of his arrogance. What makes everything more complex in these scenes is the attitude of others – those who tell him to be insincere in order to be successful in politics, and those who try to use the people's feelings for their own power and self-interest.

'Coriolanus' staged in modern dress.

Script

Act II, Scene 2

The Capitol

Enter two Officers, to lay cushions

FIRST OFFICER: Come, come, they are almost here. How many stand for consulships?

SECOND OFFICER: Three, they say: but 'tis thought of every one Coriolanus will carry it.

FIRST OFFICER: That's a brave fellow; but he's vengeance proud, and loves not the common people.

SECOND OFFICER: Faith, there had been many great men that have flattered the people, who ne'er loved them; and there be many that they have loved, they know not wherefore: so that, if they love they know not why, they hate upon no better a ground: therefore, for Coriolanus neither to care whether they love or hate him manifests the true knowledge he has in their disposition; and out of his noble carelessness lets them plainly see't.

FIRST OFFICER: He seeks their hate with greater devotion than they can render it him; and leaves nothing undone that may fully discover him their opposite. Now, to seem to affect the malice and displeasure of the people is as bad as that which he dislikes, to flatter them for their love.

SECOND OFFICER: He hath deserved worthily of his country: and his ascent is not by such easy degrees as those who, having been supple and courteous to the people, bonneted, without any further deed to have them at all, into their estimation and report: but he hath so planted his honours in their eyes, and his actions in their hearts, that for their tongues to be silent, and not confess so much, were a kind of ingrateful injury.

FIRST OFFICER: No more of him; he is a worthy man: make way, they are coming.

A sennet. Enter Cominius the consul, Menenius, Coriolanus, Senators, Sicinius and Brutus. The Senators take their places; the Tribunes take their places by themselves. Coriolanus stands

MENENIUS: Remains the point of this our after-meeting,
To gratify his noble service that
Hath thus stood for his country: therefore, please you,
Most reverend and grave elders, to desire
The present consul, and last general
In our well-found successes, to report

A little of that worthy work perform'd
By Caius Marcius Coriolanus, whom
We met here both to thank and to remember
With honours like himself.

FIRST SENATOR: Speak, good Cominius:
Leave nothing out for length, and make us think
Rather our state's defective for requital
Than we to stretch it out.

To the Tribunes

Masters o' the people,
We do request your kindest ears, and after,
Your loving motion toward the common body,
To yield what passes here.

SICINIUS: We are convented
Upon a pleasing treaty, and have hearts
Inclinable to honour and advance
The theme of our assembly.

BRUTUS: Which the rather
We shall be blest to do, if he remember
A kinder value of the people than
He hath hereto prized them at.

MENENIUS: That's off, that's off;
I would you rather had been silent. Please you
To hear Cominius speak?

BRUTUS: Most willingly;
But yet my caution was more pertinent
Than the rebuke you give it.

MENENIUS: He loves your people
But tie him not to be their bedfellow.
Worthy Cominius, speak.

Coriolanus offers to go away

Nay, keep your place.

FIRST SENATOR: Sit, Coriolanus; never shame to hear
What you have nobly done.

CORIOLANUS: Your Honour's pardon:
I had rather have my wounds to heal again
Than hear say how I got them.

BRUTUS: Sir, I hope
My words disbench'd you not.

CORIOLANUS: No, sir: yet oft,
When blows have made me stay, I fled from words.
You soothed not, therefore hurt not: but your people,
I love them as they weigh.

MENENIUS: Pray now, sit down.

CORIOLANUS: I had rather have one scratch my head i' the sun
When the alarum were struck than idly sit
To hear my nothings monster'd.

Exit

MENENIUS: Masters of the people,
Your multiplying spawn how can he flatter –
That's thousand to one good one – when you now see
He had rather venture all his limbs for honour
Than one on's ears to hear it? Proceed, Cominius.

COMINIUS: I shall lack voice: the deeds of Coriolanus
Should not be utter'd feebly. It is held
That valour is the chiefest virtue, and
Most dignifies the haver: if it be,
The man I speak of cannot in the world
Be singly counterpoised. At sixteen years,
When Tarquin made a head for Rome, he fought
Beyond the mark of others, when he drove
The bristled lips before him: he bestrid
An o'er-press'd Roman and i' the consul's view
Slew three opposers: Tarquin's self he met,
And struck him on his knee: in that day's feats,
He proved best man i' the field, and for his meed
Was brow-bound with the oak. His pupil age
Man-enter'd thus, he waxed like a sea,
And in the brunt of seventeen battles since
He lurch'd all swords of the garland. For this last,
Before and in Corioli, let me say,
I cannot speak him home: he stopp'd the fliers;
And by his rare example made the coward
Turn terror into sport so men obey'd.
He was a thing of blood, whose every motion
Was timed with dying cries: alone he enter'd
The mortal gate of the city, aidless came off,
And with a sudden reinforcement struck
Corioli like a planet: now all's his:
When, by and by, the din of war gan pierce
His ready sense; then straight his doubled spirit
Re-quicken'd what in flesh was fatigate,
And to the battle came he; where he did
Run reeking o'er the lives of men, as if
'Twere a perpetual spoil: and till we call'd
Both field and city ours, he never stood
To ease his breast with panting.

MENENIUS: Worthy man!

FIRST SENATOR: He cannot but with measure fit the honours
Which we devise him.

COMINIUS: Our spoils he kick'd at,
And look'd upon things precious as they were
The common muck of the world: he covets less
Than misery itself would give; rewards
His deeds with doing them, and is content
To spend the time to end it.

MENENIUS: He's right noble:
Let him be call'd for.

FIRST SENATOR: Call Coriolanus.

OFFICER: He doth appear.

Re-enter Coriolanus

MENENIUS: The senate, Coriolanus, are well pleased
To make thee consul.

CORIOLANUS: I do owe them still
My life and services.

MENENIUS: It then remains
That you do speak to the people.

CORIOLANUS: I do beseech you,
Let me o'erleap that custom, for I cannot
Put on the gown, stand naked and entreat them,
For my wounds' sake, to give their suffrage: please you
That I may pass this doing.

SICINIUS: Sir, the people
Must have their voices; neither will they bate
One jot of ceremony.

MENENIUS: Put them not to't:
Pray you, go fit you to the custom and
Take to you, as your predecessors have,
Your honour with your form.

CORIOLANUS: It is a part
That I shall blush in acting, and might well
Be taken from the people.

BRUTUS: Mark you that?

CORIOLANUS: To brag unto them, thus I did, and thus;
Show them the unaching scars which I should hide,
As if I had received them for the hire
Of their breath only!

MENENIUS: Do not stand upon't.
We recommend to you, tribunes of the people,
Our purpose to them: and to our noble consul
Wish we all joy and honour.

SENATORS: To Coriolanus come all joy and honour!

Flourish of cornets. Exeunt all but Sicinius and Brutus

BRUTUS: You see how he intends to use the people.

SICINIUS: May they perceive's intent! He will require them,
As if he did contemn what he requested
Should be in them to give.

BRUTUS: Come, we'll inform them
Of our proceedings here: on the marketplace,
I know, they do attend us.

Exeunt

Act II, Scene 3

The Forum

Enter seven or eight Citizens

FIRST CITIZEN: Once, if he do require our voices, we ought not to deny him.

SECOND CITIZEN: We may, sir, if we will.

THIRD CITIZEN: We have power in ourselves to do it, but it is a power that we
have no power to do; for if he show us his wounds and tell
us his deeds, we are to put our tongues into those wounds
and speak for them; so, if he tell us his noble deeds, we
must also tell him our noble acceptance of them. Ingratitude
is monstrous, and for the multitude to be ingrateful, were
to make a monster of the multitude: of the which we being
members, should bring ourselves to be monstrous members.

SECOND CITIZEN: Are you all resolved to give your voices? But that's no matter,
the greater part carries it. I say, if he would incline to the
people, there was never a worthier man.

Enter Coriolanus in a gown of humility, with Menenius

Here he comes, and in the gown of humility: mark his
behaviour. We are not to stay all together, but to
come by him where he stands, by ones, by twos, and
by threes.

ALL: Content, content.

Exeunt Citizens

MENENIUS: O sir, you are not right: have you not known
The worthiest men have done't?

CORIOLANUS: What must I say?
'I pray, sir' – Plague upon't! I cannot bring
My tongue to such a pace: – 'Look, sir, my wounds!
I got them in my country's service, when
Some certain of your brethren roar'd and ran
From the noise of our own drums.'

MENENIUS:	O me, the gods!
	You must not speak of that: you must desire them
	To think upon you.
CORIOLANUS:	Think upon me! hang 'em!
MENENIUS:	You'll mar all:
	I'll leave you: pray you, speak to 'em, I pray you,
	In wholesome manner.

Exit

CORIOLANUS:	Bid them wash their faces
	And keep their teeth clean.

Re-enter two of the Citizens

So, here comes a brace.

Re-enter a third Citizen

You know the cause, sir, of my standing here.

THIRD CITIZEN:	We do, sir; tell us what hath brought you to't.
CORIOLANUS:	Mine own desert.
SECOND CITIZEN:	Your own desert!
CORIOLANUS:	Ay, but not mine own desire.
THIRD CITIZEN:	How not your own desire?
CORIOLANUS:	No, sir, 'twas never my desire yet to trouble the poor with begging.
THIRD CITIZEN:	You must think, if we give you any thing, we hope to gain by you.
CORIOLANUS:	Well then, I pray, your price o' the consulship?
FIRST CITIZEN:	The price is to ask it kindly.
CORIOLANUS:	Kindly! Sir, I pray, let me ha't: I have wounds to show you, which shall be yours in private. Your good voice, sir; what say you?
SECOND CITIZEN:	You shall ha' it, worthy sir.
CORIOLANUS:	A match, sir. There's in all two worthy voices begged. I have your alms: adieu.
THIRD CITIZEN:	But this is something odd.
SECOND CITIZEN:	An 'twere to give again, – but 'tis no matter.

Exeunt the three Citizens
Re-enter two other Citizens

CORIOLANUS:	Pray you now, if it may stand with the tune of your voices that I may be consul, I have here the customary gown.
FOURTH CITIZEN:	You have deserved nobly of your country, and you have not deserved nobly.
CORIOLANUS:	Your enigma?

FOURTH CITIZEN: You have been a scourge to her enemies, you have
been a rod to her friends; you have not indeed loved the
common people.

CORIOLANUS: You should account me the more virtuous that I have
not been common in my love. I will, sir, flatter my sworn brother,
the people, to earn a dearer estimation of them; 'tis a condition
they account gentle: and since the wisdom of their choice is rather
to have my hat than my heart, I will practise the insinuating nod
and be off to them most counterfeitly. Therefore, I beseech you I
may be consul.

FIFTH CITIZEN: We hope to find you our friend; and therefore give you our
voices heartily.

FOURTH CITIZEN: You have received many wounds for your country.

CORIOLANUS: I will not seal your knowledge with showing them.
I will make much of your voices, and so trouble you
no further.

BOTH CITIZENS: The gods give you joy, sir, heartily!

Exeunt

CORIOLANUS: Most sweet voices!
Better it is to die, better to starve,
Than crave the hire which first we do deserve.
Why in this woolvish toge should I stand here,
To beg of Hob and Dick, that do appear?
Custom calls me to't. Rather than fool it so,
Let the high office and the honour go
To one that would do thus. I am half through;
The one part suffer'd, the other will I do.

Re-enter three Citizens more

Here come more voices.
Your voices: for your voices I have fought;
Watch'd for your voices; for your voices bear
Of wounds two dozen odd; battle thrice six
I have seen and heard of; for your voices have
Done many things, some less, some more your voices:
Indeed I would be consul.

SIXTH CITIZEN: He has done nobly, and cannot go without any honest
man's voice.

SEVENTH CITIZEN: Therefore let him be consul: the gods give him joy,
and make him good friend to the people!

ALL CITIZENS: Amen, amen. God save thee, noble consul!

Exeunt

CORIOLANUS: Worthy voices!

Re-enter Menenius, with Brutus and Sicinius

MENENIUS: You have stood your limitation; and the tribunes
Endue you with the people's voice: remains
That, in the official marks invested, you
Anon do meet the senate.

CORIOLANUS: Is this done?

SICINIUS: The custom of request you have discharged:
The people do admit you, and are summon'd
To meet anon, upon your approbation.

CORIOLANUS: Where? at the senate-house?

SICINIUS: There, Coriolanus.

CORIOLANUS: May I change these garments?

SICINIUS: You may, sir.

CORIOLANUS: That I'll straight do; and, knowing myself again,
Repair to the senate-house.

MENENIUS: I'll keep you company. Will you along?

BRUTUS: We stay here for the people.

SICINIUS: Fare you well.

Exeunt Coriolanus and Menenius

He has it now, and by his looks methink
'Tis warm at 's heart.

BRUTUS: With a proud heart he wore his humble weeds.
Will you dismiss the people?

Re-enter Citizens

SICINIUS: How now, my masters! have you chose this man?

FIRST CITIZEN: He has our voices, sir.

BRUTUS: We pray the gods he may deserve your loves.

SECOND CITIZEN: Amen, sir: to my poor unworthy notice,
He mock'd us when he begg'd our voices.

THIRD CITIZEN: Certainly
He flouted us downright.

FIRST CITIZEN: No, 'tis his kind of speech: he did not mock us.

SECOND CITIZEN: Not one amongst us, save yourself, but says
He used us scornfully: he should have show'd us
His marks of merit, wounds received for's country.

SICINIUS: Why, so he did, I am sure.

CITIZENS: No, no; no man saw 'em.

THIRD CITIZEN: He said he had wounds, which he could show in private;
And with his hat, thus waving it in scorn,
'I would be consul,' says he: 'aged custom,
But by your voices, will not so permit me;

Your voices therefore.' When we granted that,
Here was 'I thank you for your voices: thank you:
Your most sweet voices: now you have left your voices,
I have no further with you.' Was not this mockery?

SICINIUS: Why either were you ignorant to see't,
Or, seeing it, of such childish friendliness
To yield your voices?

BRUTUS: Could you not have told him
As you were lesson'd, when he had no power,
But was a petty servant to the state,
He was your enemy?

SICINIUS: Thus to have said,
As you were fore-advised, had touch'd his spirit
Or else it would have gall'd his surly nature.
You should have ta'en the advantage of his choler
And pass'd him unelected.

BRUTUS: Did you perceive
He did solicit you in free contempt
When he did need your loves, and do you think
That his contempt shall not be bruising to you,
When he hath power to crush? Why, had your bodies
No heart among you? or had you tongues to cry
Against the rectorship of judgment?

THIRD CITIZEN: He's not confirm'd; we may deny him yet.

SECOND CITIZEN: And will deny him:
I'll have five hundred voices of that sound.

FIRST CITIZEN: I twice five hundred and their friends to piece 'em.

BRUTUS: Get you hence instantly, and tell those friends,
They have chose a consul that will from them take
Their liberties; make them of no more voice
Than dogs that are as often beat for barking
As therefore kept to do so.

SICINIUS: Let them assemble,
And on a safer judgment all revoke
Your ignorant election; enforce his pride,
And his old hate unto you; besides, forget not
With what contempt he wore the humble weed,
How in his suit he scorn'd you; but your loves,
Thinking upon his services, took from you
The apprehension of his present portance,
Which most gibingly, ungravely, he did fashion
After the inveterate hate he bears you.

BRUTUS: Lay
A fault on us, your tribunes; that we laboured,

No impediment between, but that you must
Cast your election on him.

SICINIUS: Say, you chose him
More after our commandment than as guided
By your own true affections, and that your minds,
Preoccupied with what you rather must do
Than what you should, made you against the grain
To voice him consul: lay the fault on us.

BRUTUS: Ay, spare us not. Say we read lectures to you.
How youngly he began to serve his country,
How long continued, and what stock he springs of.

SICINIUS: But you have found,
Scaling his present bearing with his past,
That he's your fixed enemy, and revoke
Your sudden approbation.

BRUTUS: Say, you n'er had done't –
Harp on that still – but by our putting on;
And presently, when you have drawn your number,
Repair to the Capitol.

ALL: We will so: almost all
Repent in their election.

Exeunt Citizens

SICINIUS: To the Capitol, come:
We will be there before the stream o' the people;
And this shall seem, as partly 'tis, their own,
Which we have goaded onward.

Exeunt

Postscript

Purpose
- humour at Coriolanus's struggle to overcome his own feelings
- exploration of political behaviour

Effects
- humour at Coriolanus's reluctance to play politics
- humour at other people's efforts to persuade him to play the political game
- insight into deceit, pretence and self-interest

Devices
- verbal irony
- dramatic irony
- asides
- repeat situations

Glossary

consulship	one of the most important offices in Roman government
sennet	ceremonial trumpet signal of entry
gratify	give grateful thanks for
convented	both agreed
pertinent	apt, appropriate
disbench'd	get up as if to leave
than one on's ears	than someone as young as he
Tarquin	leader of the enemy army
meed	deserved reward
brow-bound with the oak	honoured with an oak-leaf crown
pupil age	youth
man-enter'd	early manhood
Corioli	the city Caius Martius conquered
gan	began to
fatigate	fatigued, tired
covets	envies and wants to possess
give their suffrage	elect by vote
bate	reduce, omit
contemn	despise
gown of humility	white gown worn by candidates (candidatus = Latin for white-gowned)
alms	charitable offerings
limitation	test
approbation	approval
gall'd	injured
choler	anger
weed	garment
portance	conduct, behaviour
gibingly	sneeringly
ungravely	not seriously
inveterate	deep-rooted, settled in habit

Close-up on language

1 Which words does Cominius choose to influence the emotions of his audience?

2 Which words show Coriolanus's dislike of the plebs?

3 Which words show his struggle to do what he has been told to do?

4 Which words show his pride in his achievements?

5 Which words show him becoming increasingly confident at playing the game of dealing with the common people?

'A Midsummer Night's Dream' performed by The Royal Shakespeare Company, 1995. Puck and First Fairy in a dramatic pose.

Understanding character

Getting into thoughts and feelings

When Coriolanus says "Bid them wash their faces / And keep their teeth clean", what he says is what he feels – that he thinks the people are filthy and beneath his contempt. On the other hand, when he says "Your voices: for your voices I have fought" he does not mean it. He says it because it is what the people want to hear, and he has learned that he must not say what he thinks and feels if he is to get their support.

Look at other moments where a character reacts to a situation or to someone else and see what the character may be thinking or feeling at that moment.

1 What is in Menenius's mind at these points?

> "To gratify his noble service that
> Hath thus stood for his country"
>
> "That's off, that's off"
>
> "Pray now, sit down."

2 What is in Cominius's mind at these points?

> "The man I speak of cannot in the world
> Be singly counterpoised."
>
> "he covets less
> Than misery itself would give"

3 What are Sicinius and Brutus thinking at these points?

> "Which the rather
> We shall be blest to do, if he remember
> A kinder value of the people than
> He hath hereto prized them at."
>
> "my caution was more pertinent"
>
> "the people
> Must have their voices; neither will they bate
> One jot of ceremony."

4 What is Coriolanus thinking and feeling at these points?

> *Coriolanus offers to go away*
>
> "I love them as they weigh"
>
> "please you
> That I may pass this doing."
>
> "As if I had received them for the hire
> Of their breath only!"

5 What are the people's attitudes and feelings at these points?

> THIRD CITIZEN: "It is a power that we have no power to do"
>
> SECOND CITIZEN: "I say, if he would incline to the people, there was never a worthier man."

Personal response

1 What do you feel about Coriolanus's statement that he does not want to put on the gown of humility and beg the common people for their votes?

2 How would you advise Coriolanus to be successful in winning people's votes?

Understanding performance

Staging and directing

1 What should the actor playing Menenius do at these points?

> "Pray now, sit down."
>
> "The senate, Coriolanus, are well pleased
> To make thee consul."

2 What should the actors playing Sicinius and Brutus do at these points?

> "Mark you that?"
>
> "Come, we'll inform them
> Of our proceedings here: on the marketplace,
> I know, they do attend us."

3 What should the actor playing Coriolanus do at these points?

> SICINIUS: "Sir, the people
> Must have their voices; neither will they bate
> One jot of ceremony."
>
> "To brag unto them, thus I did, and thus;
> Show them the unaching scars which I should hide,
> As if I had received them for the hire
> Of their breath only!"

Practical work

Solo or in pairs

1 Read Cominius's speech in praise of Coriolanus's qualities

  • as a friend, fondly recalling his action

2　Read Coriolanus's speech that begins "'I pray, sir' – Plague upon't!"

- bringing out his contempt for the words he is being asked to use
- bringing out his contempt for the people he is being asked to be polite to.

3　Design a theatre poster or video cover showing Coriolanus bloodstained after the battle, and standing in a white gown asking for the people's votes.

In groups

1　**Hot seat**

　a　Put Coriolanus in the hot seat and question him about his feelings before and after asking for the people's votes.

　b　Put Sicinius and Brutus in the hot seat and ask them why they persuaded the people to change their minds – and why they told them to say that Sicinius and Brutus had encouraged them to vote for Coriolanus.

　c　Put Menenius in the hot seat and question him about Coriolanus. Ask him how easy it is to deal with him.

2　**Tableau talkback**

　The group freezes in a tableau of the scene in the senate or on the street. The questioner walks around the figures in the tableau and asks what different characters think about the situation.

3　Perform the scene where Coriolanus stands in the street to ask for votes. Bring out his unwillingness to do this, and his increasing confidence as the scene goes on.

Social, cultural and historical aspects

1　What events in our society and in our time could be seen as similar to this procedure for electing a consul?

2　What devices do you notice that could be used today by someone trying to influence the public?

Coriolanus takes centre stage.